Faint Whispers f

The archaeological environment surrounding the Temple of Apollo at Didyma

Technical editing: J&M

Copy editing: Izabela Miszczak

On the cover: Fallen columns at the back of the Temple of Apollo.

ISBN: 978-83-953130-2-8 (ePub)
ISBN: 978-83-953130-3-5 (Kindle eBook)
ISBN: 978-83-953130-4-2 (paperback)

Publisher: ASLAN Publishing House

Contact: contact@turkisharchaeonews.net
FaceBook: http://facebook.com/turkisharchaeonews
WWW: http://turkisharchaeonews.net/

Second Edition: March 2019

Glenn Maffia

Faint Whispers from the Oracle

The archaeological environment surrounding the Temple of Apollo at Didyma

Contents

Preface	vii
About the Author	ix
Introduction	1
An Historic Walk along the Sacred Way	7
Engravings at Apollo Temple	15
The Stadium of Apollo's Light	23
Immersed within the Baths	31
Revealing the Theatre	37
A mystery waiting to speak	43
A curious alienation	51
A Temple that whispers from our past	55
Artemis' wishing well	65
A confusion of aims	71
Hidden background of the Archaeologists work	77

The covenant of Apollo 85

When the earth convulses 95

Projection of imagination 101

Build in Light 107

Meeting at the Miletus Museum 111

The Exchange of Populations House 115

Pushing the territory of the 'faux pas' 121

The Spring of Apollo bursts forth 125

A glimmer of light shines forth 131

Photographic Appendices 135

Bibliography 141

Preface

Naturally my intention on this subject of the archaeology that surrounds the elegant Hellenistic Temple of Apollo, standing in the small resort town of Didim upon Turkey's Aegean coastline, is not only to extol the excitement of the recent finds made by the archaeologists from the Martin Luther University of Halle in Germany, but also an attempt to galvanize the Turkish authorities into sanctioning a thorough excavation of this most important site in ancient Asia Minor. For all within paradise is not perfect. Therefore my text, I trust you find, shall read as panegyric to the ennobled virtues of ancient Greece and Rome and the resourceful endeavours of the archaeologists engaged in disclosing our ancient heritage. Whilst yearning that my constructive criticism on the lack of development of this fascinating site shall be taken accordingly, and not as a polemic devoid of sensitivity.

The second edition of the book reflects important developments that occurred around and within the extensive archaeological site of the Temple throughout 2018.

Despite the astounding continuance of finds unearthed by the German-led archaeologists and the encouraging noises emanating from the Ministry of Culture and Tourism in Ankara, no discernable shift in the stifling inertia which encircles the Temple locally has been forthcoming. Quite the contrary actually, as new buildings appear in a profusion to 'conform' (I use that word liberally) to an article of legislation concerning the Certificates of Habitation required for all building within the Republic of Turkey.

Needless to say, no archaeology has been noticeable in, around or beneath these new buildings. This all rather echoes a comment I made recently to an article investigating the illegal trade of ancient artefacts published in one of the daily Turkish newspapers; 'A massive problem in a culturally rich country which has a widespread disregard of cultural artifacts'.

I am hoping that I may be of some little help in assisting the intended aim of the Turkish Government to protect and display such an encompassing cultural heritage in a manner befitting its magnificent importance.

I have attempted to ensure that this text is encompassing to all readers from all backgrounds, steering away from a singularly academic inclination which may prove too cold to those with an avid interest in 'popular' history. I hope I have come somewhere near to succeeding with that intent.

May you read, cogitate and then espouse your feelings.

Glenn Maffia. Didim, February 2019

About the Author

Originating from London, Glenn Maffia deeply appreciates that he was fortunate enough to have the availability of that city's surfeit of magnificent, and free, Museums and Art Galleries at his disposal throughout his youth. An opportunity he hungrily embraced.

He attended Art School where he graduated with a Diploma in Graphic Design, before later enrolling with the Open University, whilst he was working in the fledgling computer industry. His interdisciplinary studies included; 'Victorian Britain: An arts foundation course', 'Modern Art and Modernism', 'Art in Fifteenth Century Italy', 'The Enlightenment', 'Philosophy of the Arts', 'Culture and Belief in Europe 1450-1600', 'Art, Society and Religion' and 'Fifth Century Athens: Democracy and City State'. He graduated with a Bachelor of Arts (Honours) degree and a Diploma in European Humanities.

Glenn was first attracted to Didim in Turkey when seeing a solitary photograph of the Temple of Apollo upon the pages of a holiday brochure early in 1996. After his two week visit, which also saw him venture to Priene and Miletus, his interest was ignited enough for him to enquire further into the history of this tiny corner of the world nestling upon the Aegean Sea.

Glenn emigrated to Didim in 2003, since when he has been a regular contributor and columnist for two English language local newspapers, the 'Didymian' (2005-2006) and 'Voices' (2006-present).

Introduction

A brief history of where we are

Since the nineteen-sixties the German Archaeological Institute has received permission from the Turkish Government to search for any evidence surrounding the greatly documented Temple of Apollo at Didyma. The meaning of the word 'Didyma', the ancient name of the settlement, in ancient Greek is 'twin' or 'twins'. Such is the intensity of the reams of writing upon the Temple that I have chosen to concentrate on the surrounding environment in an attempt to flesh out the picture in one's mind's eye of what we would have been confronted by if we could have walked this land during its halcyon days. Therefore, rather than re-iterating that which more eminent historian's pens have, in their educated hands, traced upon many thousands of pages, I shall refrain from detailed analysis of the Temple itself. Save for an interesting detail in the Pronaos which I have never encountered previously on the printed page; probably because it is so humanly banal, though that, to me, lends a very informative trait.

The mathematically mellifluous harmonies of the Temple's design upon a novel plan of three distinctly separate levels would have elevated its prestige onto the list of the Seven Wonders of the World if only it were complete. Though the structure was never entirely finished; the columns along its southern stylobate are the missing element in this magnificent example of humankind's endeavour to trace the rhythms of beauty. The gift of finding something incomplete does have the benefit of lending itself to how the process of construction developed over time. A particular example of this at

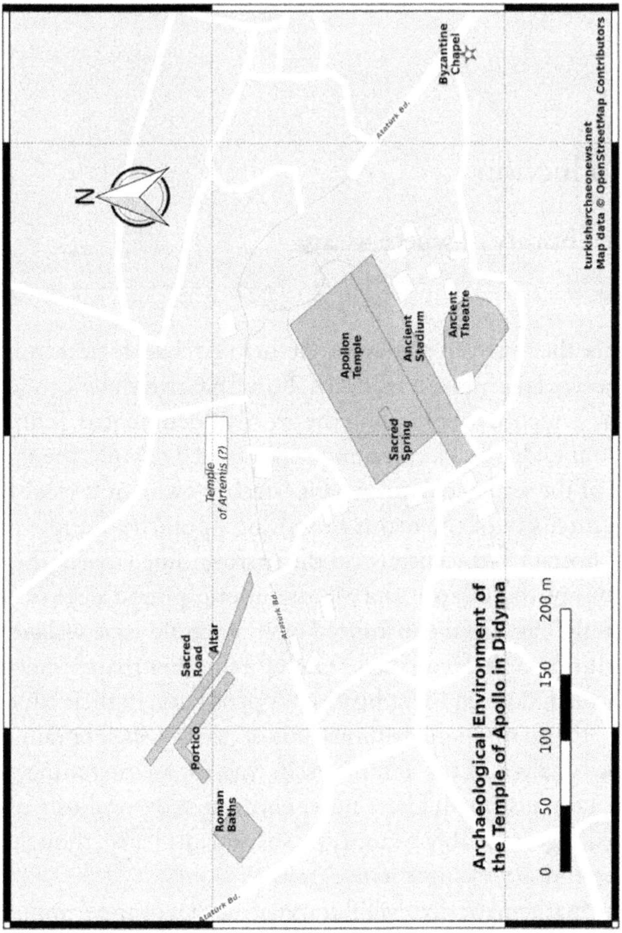

Fig. 1. Archaeological Environment of the Temple of Apollo in Didyma.

Didyma can be seen quite clearly upon the three columns which remain standing. The twin columns holding aloft a segment of entablature have been completed with the adornment of some

Fig. 2. Surroundings of the Temple of Apollo.

exquisite fluting descending from its Ionian capitals, whereas the column standing defiantly alone upon the southern stylobate is the lasting legacy of the incomplete section of the Temple. We can observe here that its surface is devoid of any fluting apart from the section just beneath the capital, where it is possible to adjudicate that a column was initially raised and then, and only then, given the fine finish of the fluting. That this design was a unique plan for an Archaic, and later a Hellenistic, temple is reasoned by considering the geography of the land upon which the earliest shrine to the god Apollo was constructed. The original buildings were probably nothing more than wooden edifices. It nonetheless resided within a place which was always sacred to Apollo; a source of a fresh spring surrounded by a laurel grove. That this rested within a geographical depression would eventually, in time, culminate in spectacular and breathtaking architectural three-level design we see to this day. A plan that is quite unmatched in any later sophisticated temple. The modest initial structure was instigated before any Ionian ever set foot upon this soil, for Apollo is not from the Greek Pantheon but an Anatolian deity, as attested by some inscriptions from various Hittite sources where he is referred to as Apulunas. Pausanias states that a temple dedicated to Apollo, renowned for the ability to prophesize, was already in existence before the Greek colonisation during the 10th century BCE, though only he claims that, and no further evidence has been established.

Fig. 3. Surroundings of the Temple of Apollo.

Fig. 4. Temple of Apollo with its three standing columns, the unfluted one can be seen on the left.

The Ionians, we can surmise from the name, came from the lands that were washed by the Sea of Ionia, between Greece and

Italy. They arrived upon these shores in the eastern Aegean in the 8th century BCE, via Athens who probably gave them refuge from the warlike Lacedaemonians, better known as the Spartans, before shipping them off to do the Athenian bidding in trading posts strewn throughout the Mediterranean and the Black Sea coasts. Thus they arrived, one of so many peoples to settle in this land, in which conflict and the spilling of blood were the mere bywords of survival. History can never have clearly defined edges, it rather melts one into another, and there is always a blurring during these passages of time. I trust that you shall hold to that thought as you travel through these pages.

An Historic Walk along the Sacred Way

Archaeology, since Charles Newton (1857/8) until the present, has continued to reveal important and fascinating evidence of the practices of religious observation duly performed in honouring the god Apollo at Didyma. One of the most intriguing facets being that of the procession from the Apollo Delphinion in Miletus along the Sacred Way to Apollo's sanctuary at Didyma.

There once existed a prestigious Milesian cult association instrumental in the rituals surrounding the pagan deity of Apollo, named the 'Molpoi' (Singers). The god's many accoutrements included that of music after all. An inscription dated from c.100 BCE records a cult law from this society, upon which is included a tract from 479/478 BCE, just after the defeat of the Persians at the Battle of Mykale. It informs us of the procession from Miletus along the route of the Sacred Way, specifying the precise ceremonies and venues which were performed upon the way. Naturally, some rites would have been performed once they arrived at Didyma, though these are not recounted upon this piece of evidence, with the exception of laying a 'gyllos,' i.e. a basket of donations or dedications, at the ruined doors of the archaic temple. The Archaic Temple was destroyed by the Persians in 494 BCE, though the cult remained active throughout the intervening period before the construction of the Hellenistic temple began.

This cult decree from the Molpoi plots their route across the undulating hills, valleys and meadows with such precision that it has been possible to locate many of their locations for sacrificial offerings and hymn singing. From the south gate of Miletus— the only leading landward in ancient times— the procession led over

Fig. 5. The map of the Sacred Way.

initially flat land before rising over the barrier of hills running from west to east along the Milesian peninsula. The German archaeologist Theodor Wiegand postulates that the route passed through a wood (drymos) and upwards, it was just before the pinnacle of the "height" (akron) that the procession paused in a meadow (leimon) to sing their hymns to the nymphs. From there the road went over the brow of the hill and into a ravine called Dyo Bryseis (Two Springs) descending from the "height", around another hill before reaching the sea just north of Panormos, modern-day Mavişehir, three and a half kilometres north-west of Didyma. Thereafter they made stops at two unidentified places before arriving at the Chares group of statues, now in the British Museum, which lined the Sacred Way before the temenos (sacred enclosure) limits of Didyma. Finally, they arrived at the entrance to the enclosure of the Temple of Apollo. This procession would have been an integral part of the festival to Apollo in providing entertainment for the crowds as they wended their way towards the Temple. One could quite easily imagine the excitement gradually building into a crescendo of noise; the musicians with their assortment of wind instruments, turning the hot still air shrill, the cithara playing and the many drums pounding out an incessant rhythm. Dancers would have weaved in and out between the instrumentalists. Though the manner of their dances has been consigned to the past, never recorded, forever lost to us today.

Fig. 6. The excavated fragment of the Sacred Way near the Temple of Apollo.

Along the length of the entire road there would have been the occasional statues, monumental tombs, the sarcophagi encasing affluent Milesians and places where those in the procession could rest. Indeed, one of these resting places was excavated as recently as

Fig. 7. Statues of the Branchids from the Sacred Way, now in Room 13 at the British Museum.

1985 some 4km south of the modern village of Akköy. The seductive name of the 'Terrace with the Sphinx' graphically alludes to what was found there. These places of archaeological interest intensified the nearer one approached the temenos of Didyma. At the last sanctuary before the temenos, labelled Chares upon the map, the British archaeologist Charles Newton found a group of statues of the Branchids (prophets/priests) and a reclining lion whilst excavating between 1857/58. Permission was sought and received from the Ottoman authorities to ship these artefacts to Britain. One can today view them in Room 13 at the British Museum. Four statues remained and are housed at the Miletus Museum. Not everyone walked the entire Sacred Way; some took a ship from Miletus along the coast to the small port at Panormos and then proceeded on foot the short distance to Didyma. The boundary of the Didymaean temenos was around three hundred metres from the Temple itself, a huge area which afforded sanctuary (sanctified, as in purified). Another Molpoi inscription alludes to gates (thyrai) at Didyma in the fifth century BCE, though this may well be a reference to the entrance of the Apollon precinct or even the Temple doors themselves. Nonetheless, in c.100/101 CE, when Emperor Trajan was renovating the Sacred Way, a gate, perhaps in the form of an arch, was built. In 1907 the foundations of this structure were discovered. As those in the procession entered into the area of the temenos, at least during Roman rule, they would have seen the Gymnasium and Baths to their right with the shops following a few metres further along the route. To their left, there were probably more shops and another sacred area within its own temenos. It was thought that this sacred place was an altar to Artemis, though that idea is fast losing traction as our knowledge increases. Back to the right, just after the last of the shops were passed, a location upon a ridge was dotted by fountains and wells. These, too, were once believed to be associated with Artemis though some opinions are turning towards the more prosaic necessity of having a sufficient water supply to quench the thirst of all these gathered people. Whilst as this area is also close to the Baths it is inviting to think that they fed the favourite pastime of the attendee population.

A perplexing anomaly continues to exist upon the route of the Sacred Way. From the temenos, the road progresses nearly 200 metres before turning in a dog-leg east direction some 150 metres north of the north-west corner of the Temple. It was always thought that this turn would naturally follow to the main façade of the temple. Two archaeological digs in 2014 and 2015 revealed nothing. The proposal was that they had been "robbed out"; the stone used for later constructions. Plausible, and understandable, within the intervening centuries. Though whilst we have historically insensitive inhabitants surrounding the Temple, we shall never solve this perplexing riddle.

As of writing, this area of the Sacred Way has been closed to the public for a number of years. I have persistently asked not only, "Why is it closed?", but also inquired as to when the public shall be allowed accessibility. Possibly I should be asking the question, "Why is it not open?" The archaeologists from the University of

Fig. 8. Statue of a reclining lion from the Sacred Way, now in Room 13 at the British Museum.

Fig. 9. Statues of the Branchids from the Sacred Way, now in Miletus Museum.

Fig. 10. Statues of the Sphinxes from the Sacred Way, now in Miletus Museum.

Halle, Germany, have installed some very impressive information boards; therefore they were anticipating access to be available to the public. All I have ever received is lame excuse followed by an even lamer excuse and, believe me, it becomes quite tiresome having to listen to such blatant fabrications. A local archaeologist and personal friend explained that the road is under the jurisdiction of the Museum at Miletus. Which he appears to believe explains it all. As I have never been afforded the courtesy of meeting these persons I cannot comment. Most of the tombs have been 'robbed out' ever since the very initial excavations, and probably before also, though unfortunately, the practice of dreaming of quick untold riches persists to this day. I have been approached on many occasions to reveal the whereabouts of the tombs along the road, upon which I always laconically reply, "All robbed out, years ago".

Engravings at Apollo Temple

Climbing the stairs to the vastly impressive front façade of the Temple will bring one into the Pronaos, an area allowing the petitioners to await the answers to their questions received by the god of prophecy. It was here that the priests of Apollo's shrine pulled back one of three doors between the Cresmographeion and the Adyton to deliver those cryptic words of knowledge and wisdom relayed from the prophetess deep within the holy inner sanctum to the petitioners. I shall discuss these rituals later, but first I shall focus upon the massed petitioners in the Pronaos and some curious engravings.

Carved upon the marble flagstones one can discern a multitude of circular incised graffito within which straight lines cut the circle into eight equal segments (I've counted 32, but there may be more lurking under the grime). Tour guides, always a source of dubious information, usually refer to all these graffiti as 'ichthys' Christian symbols. Granted, their identical appearance is, indeed, indisputable. Though an 'ichthys' is a symbol made from using the first letter of each word in Greek:

> ΙΧΘΥΣ (Ἰησοῦς Χριστός, Θεοῦ Υἱός, Σωτήρ.
> Latin script: Iēsous Christos, Theou Yios, Sōtēr).

The English translates as, "Jesus Christ, Son of God, Saviour". Overlaying these Greek letters upon one another results in the circle dissected by eight equal segments. Separately these initial letters also spell 'fish' in Greek, which relates to another symbol esteemed by Christians to this day, whilst also relating to Jesus' alleged occupation as a fisherman of Galilee. However, there are clues as to the true identity of the engravings. Noticeably the sheer number of them that are found to be strewn across the floor spaces of the Pronaos. None are found upon a wall for example. Surely such clandestine Christian symbols, for these were used before that religion became the dominant ideology, within a magnificent and high profile pagan temple their daring would be all the more pronounced within the eye-line of the attended people. All, though, are found upon the floor. Why?

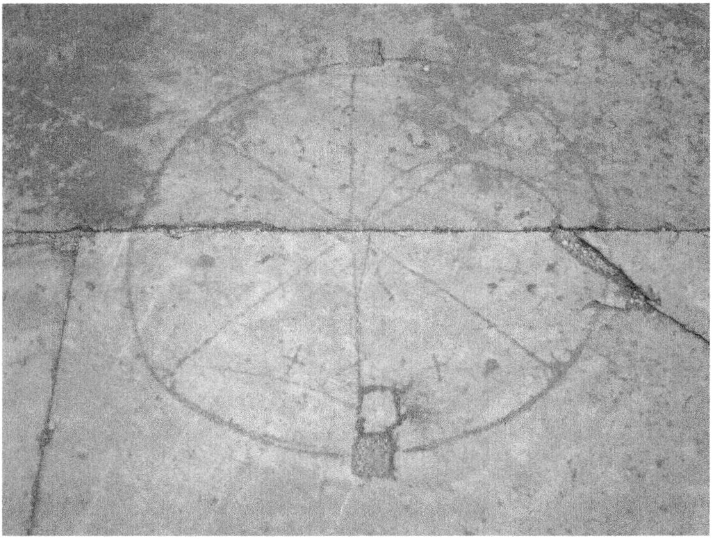

Fig. 11. Circular grafitto, carved upon the marble flagstones of the Temple of Apollo.

Simply, these deeply inscribed scratches are clearly some kind of a game, possibly played with dice and counters; a very human activity to while away the time whilst awaiting the priestess to consult the god, and then the priest scribes to arrange them into hexameter verse as all replies from Apollo were given in hexameter form at Didyma, before the great doors were opened and the pronouncements relayed to the assembled masses. We can, therefore, leave the spiritual completely out of this equation, to appreciate the very human notion of passing some dull period of time aside with something which entertains them. We all do the same ourselves. There is no requirement to 'read in' into an artefact or work of art when we really should be 'reading out' of that object. Hunt games were extremely popular in ancient times. Therefore, it appears to me, given the circularity, the games belong in that chase category. Choose for yourself whether they were Hare and Foxes, Bear and Hounds, etc., etc., etc. Closer inspection also reveals that there are distinct variations of the shapes within the circle, some of which are impressively complex. These variations in no way resemble the Christian symbol of the 'ichthys'. If any more confirmation were needed, then this game is not the only one to be inscribed upon the flagstones. Indeed, there is an extremely famous example, just to one's right once one has ascended the stairs. A very obvious precursor of backgammon, the Romans called this game 'Ludus duodecimo scriptorum'. A literal translation of this name is 'game of twelve markings' which refers to the three rows of twelve features upon the playing area. The game was played with three dice which determined the movement of the 15 pieces each player had available. Therefore, taking the human aspect as logical evidence in preference to some religious belief, or a tour guide trying to impress western tourists, we find that it contains no evidence whatsoever, we have here a clear example of how our ancestors passed the time quite convivially with their compatriots.

During the early 1900's, when a German team began to excavate the temple, under the guidance of the eminent Theodor Wiegand, a Christian Basilica was found within the Adyton (inner sanctum). It was rather hastily pulled down without too much investigation into this structure; some of the remains of this Basilica now lie to the south of the Temple lined along the Stadium track. This haste was probably due to the excitement of finding more engravings upon what was being used for the construction material for the Basilica walls. Though these incisions upon the re-used stones were nothing as trivial as the games we looked at earlier, but inscriptions which recorded the words of the Oracle. It is thought that

Fig. 12. Remains of a Christian Basilica, now moved to the south of the Temple of Apollo, along the Stadium track.

they were originally the walls of the 'Prophet's House', of which we are yet to find any trace. Or possibly from an earlier Cresmographeion set away from the Temple proper, again its whereabouts is unknown and waits to be found. The sheer number of these inscriptions has enabled the archaeologists to piece together a fairly clear picture of the rituals and social proclivities enacted over a long period. These coupled with texts discovered at Miletus continue to add clarity to our perceptions.

Meanwhile, deep within the recesses of the Adyton, three days of preparation were coming to a conclusion. The prophetess, accompanied by a high ranking civil servant of Miletus acting as her prophet, had abided by a strict "rule of complete purity", which one can infer meant sexual purity. This purity was also obtained by bathing, long held as a method of purification, and abstinence from eating for the three days, alongside performing the sacrifices which were deemed an absolute necessity to her duties. According to Iamblichus (c.250-330 CE) by the time of the 'unison' with

Fig. 13. Altar of Apollo standing directly in front of the entrance steps to the Temple of Apollo.

Apollo she, "was already possessed by the divine light". She would then have moved out onto a wooden beam, in one hand holding a rod which symbolised the rod that Apollo handed down to Branchus, the legendary founder of Didyma's oracle, and straddled the sacred well which contained the waters of the sacred spring towards the rear of the inner sanctum. There the waters would wet either the hem of her robe or her feet whilst she breathed in the emissions of sulphurous vapour emanating from the pool. There, starved of food for three days and high on the inhalation of heady fumes, she probably uttered an inane gibberish of nonsensical noises whilst the prophet stood alongside scribbling down his interpretations of her noises into hexameter verse. I am sure that none shall have any argument with the notion that a high ranking civil servant would inevitably follow his own self-interest given such a position of a religiously sanctioned authority. That it was a position only held for a single year did not prevent the same person being nominated year after year. Considering the costs involved in performing one's duties, it would have only been the very elite of Milesian society that could have afforded the role. As for the prophetess, well, we only know the name of one, Tryphosa c.200 CE, and she also belonged to a very elite Milesian family.

Fig. 14. Precursor of backgammon – game of twelve markings, carved upon the marble flagstones of the Temple of Apollo.

It depended upon who the Prophet was as to what dominant mode of expression was performed at the festivals, though this, naturally, was pronounced as if it were the express wish of Apollo himself. The inscriptions record a source of personal information, including some family trees from the Roman era. See Robinson and also Fontenrose for some translated versions. There were those who preferred the mass sacrifice of animals, the hecatomb, which is the slaughter of one hundred oxen or sheep upon the altar immediately in front of the stairway to the Temple. Another version of these physical, and costly, gifts for the god was the presentation of exquisite statues made of gold or silver at his shrine. Though others, such as Aelius Graninus Ambeibios Macer, whose career and rise to the position of a prophet is excellently recounted in Robin

Lane Fox's "Pagans and Christians", chose to call upon another of Apollo's attributes, that of the god of music. Obviously, for he was an accomplished musician himself, the words of the oracle were merely the inclinations of the prophet alone.

The Stadium of Apollo's Light

As in all ancient Greek and Roman places of dense population an area for physical sporting prowess was a prominent feature. And Didyma was an area containing a throng of humanity during the time of the festival in honour of Apollo.

The site of the Stadium was, and remains, immediately to the left of the Temple as we look upon it facing the impressive entrance and proceeds to continue along the entire length of the south-east periphery to which it is aligned. Though as the Temple's length is measured at 109.34 metres, this seems rather short when the average length of an ancient field track is normally considered to be 180 metres. Obviously, there are many exceptions and variations, but just over a hundred metres appears stunted to a surprising extreme. The only inference that one can imagine is that the field continued onwards past the present day boundary wall to the southwest and concluded somewhere under the crumbling shanty houses, which continue to be occupied to this day. As one can still see the positions of the race's starting posts at the southeast corner of the Temple, it seems logical to assume that the 'finishing line' would have been located under those dilapidated houses. Naturally, where there is a 'finish line' there would be congregated the eminent personages of the day. I fully suspect that if it were possible to perform the archaeology in this area we would find a substantial foundation of the Stadium's viewing auditorium, one I would suspect of being impressive in its size and articulation. The seating areas for the spectators along the side of the track were the steps along the south-east façade of the Temple, whilst another set, today mainly ruined, rose upon the other side.

The width of this track was particularly narrow compared to the extant one at Olympia, as it measures, approximately, a paltry 10 metres. If one searches along the preserved seating area one can still observe the vast array of etched names of attendees cut into the tall steps. Whereas it is my belief that the leading personages of Miletus and/or Rome would have dominated in the auditorium by the finishing line, these spectator's names we can observe today must have been from the lower ranks of society where the etched names would reserve a position, much as a 'season ticket' does today at sporting events. I feel that the inscriptions not being written in educated hands gives credence to this being evidence.

As for the festival of games itself there are conflicting reports of its frequency; some commentators infer that it was an annual event, whereas others state quite clearly that it occurred every four years. It is here that we must remember that the festival and games had a prolonged existence which dated back, possibly, to the initial temple in c.8th century BCE, while Pausanius argues even the 10th century BCE. Within such a timeframe it would be logical to consider the four-year cycle to be expedient in a practical nature, especially during the early years of settlement. Whereas as the cities of Achaean (Greek) Ionia became more affluent, and once eventually under Roman influence, the yearly cycle could be explained. The twelve city-states formed by the Ionians along this coastline consisted of Miletus, Priene, Myus and Samos on an island in the south, Ephesus, Colophon, Teos and Lebedus in the central region and Erythrae, Clazomenae, Phocaea, and Chios on an island in the north. These cities formed themselves into the Panionion League for self-protection in a hostile frontier. It would not be surprising if many, and probably all, sent their athletic champions to compete in the events. Miletus was generally the most wealthy and prominent city in the alliance, at least until the Romans made Ephesus their capital of 'Asia Minor', and therefore in all likelihood held sway over the other eleven cities.

As the stadium is well defined and attested, the obvious question would be to ask of the whereabouts of the always accompanying

Fig. 15. Seating of the Stadium – the steps along the southeast façade of the Temple of Apollo.

Gymnasium? The place for training for athletic events was always situated close to the 'field of battle' during the Greek period, though over the 1,200 years of transformation into the Roman period the Gymnasium was closely associated with the Roman Baths. We can still see this today, in Miletus, where the Faustina

Fig. 16. Starting posts of the Stadium at the southeast corner of the Temple of Apollo.

Baths are abutted by the Gymnasium. We have the remnants of the Roman Baths at Didyma, but looking for what is intrinsically a flat piece of ground, perhaps surrounded by a portico, is not going to register much upon the geo-phys detecting machines. I shall expand upon this in the Roman Baths chapter.

Fig. 17. Reserved seating of the Stadium.

Fig. 18. Stadium next to the Temple of Apollo.

Considering the long timescale of the existence of an important temple at Didyma, some of the sporting events would conceivably have come and gone within the fashionable vagaries of a particular age. There is however absolutely no archaeological evidence of any sporting event involving horses. Therefore expel any notions of chariot races circling the Temple, it never happened. Obviously as the track is quite well defined and its starting blocks, roughly, in place, running would certainly be a dominant feature of any games. Whilst if my theory of a spectator gallery around the finishing line is correct, then it is conceivable that boxing and/or wrestling contests would take place in or near this vicinity. One can imagine as the competitors entered the arena a tingling of excitement ripple through the crowd. The noise rising as the crowd began to recognise their champions amongst the other competitors, loosening their limbs, flexing their well-oiled muscles and shaking the stiffness out of their joints, as the crescendo of clamorous uproar went to even higher decibels. Once more the musicians would appear to further stir the excitement mounting in the throng, the brightly coloured banners were unfurled and waved upon the still air whilst the dancers, acrobats and jugglers kept the attention of people between the events. It was pure theatre. Such revelry must have continued late into the night chill as the buzz of excitement refused to decline within the breast of the multitudes. Heady on the adrenalin of euphoria and copious amounts of wine, the eateries and alcohol houses would be choked with the masses and the prostitutes in the brothels doing a roaring trade. Their attitudes towards the pleasures of the flesh unchained from a jealous and proscriptive ideology invoking an abstract, and absolutely unnatural, sense of guilt. Only, if only, we could dig down to find the dying echoes of these Dionysian raptures what a picture we could paint. It is an embarrassing shame on this town that the relevant permissions cannot be obtained to undertake a full archaeological survey of this enigmatic and fascinating site and especially these places of revelry. If nothing more, it would give us a better understanding of the size and scale of the area of habitation which once surrounded the Temple. A temple of shimmering beauty during the heat of summer; now standing in perverse isolation, slowly drowning beneath the ever-encroaching discoloured concrete apartment blocks and business ventures of questionable ethics.

Fig. 19. Dilapidated houses, most probably situated over the finishing line of the Stadium.

Immersed within the Baths

Unfortunately the excavation of the Roman Baths (Thermae) was long completed before I turned my attention to the study of the Temple environment. Whilst to those of us who are interested and inquisitive, for some reason, which remains stubborn in not being forthcoming, are forbidden access to the area. Therefore most of the information I have is of a 'secondary source' nature.

Fig. 20. Roman Baths on the Sacred Way.

The Baths are situated to the left of the Sacred Way looking from the Temple conclusion of the road, though the structure is obscured by the trees when viewing from the railings. It may be worth your while to buy yourself a cold drink at the newly opened restaurant and sip it upon the balcony at the back of the building. The Roman Baths of the so-named 'serial type' were of a similar design, though certainly not of size, consisting of a changing area (Apodyterium), a cold section (Frigidarium), a lukewarm section (Tepidarium), a hot section (Caldarium) and finally, in the larger baths, a 'hell-high heat' section (Sudatorium). Didyma's Baths did not possess the later, which may give a clue to its dating that I shall discuss below. The larger baths complexes included areas where one could indulge in some form of physical activity; the palaestra (exercise area), plunge or swimming pools depending upon the size of the complex and a gymnasium. The palaestra or gymnasium at Didyma is indicated by a doorway leading to the north of the Baths. The archaeologists discovered a rectangular section of open land with evidence that a colonnaded structure once covered the perimeter. The heat for the Baths was produced from a number of strategically placed furnaces around the edges of the structure, and it was channelled by a network of terracotta or lead pipes beneath the raised floors; the famous hypocaust system. Just to the south of the Baths, upon a ridge, were located many wells and fountains; therefore the supply of water for the leisure centre of Didyma was close at hand and plentiful. The Baths were truly at the hub of Roman life; a place not only to relax and occupy one's self with the fastidious obsession to cleanliness but also a centre to discuss business deals, political intrigues and just plain old gossip. Roman life, it seems, would have ceased without such a facility. It appears that the preferred route after paying one's entrance fee would have been to at first bring out a sweat in the exercise area before passing through to the tepidarium, which acclimatized one to the heat then awaiting him or her in the caldarium. When in the caldarium the heat would further sweat out the dirt and grime from the pores of the body. It was then that an attendant, usually a slave, though in the more upmarket Baths a professional masseur, would apply olive oil onto the customer's flesh before scraping off the oil and any dead skin cells with an instrument called a strigil; a curved shaped knife with a furrow running along its blade to collect the oil, sweat and grime. Thus thoroughly cleaned the customer would return to the tepidarium, no doubt stopping to chat about topics of the day with others assembled there whilst cooling down before entering the frigidarium to further cool the body and to immerse oneself into a plunge pool to close the pores of the skin. Therefore, cleaned, refreshed and, after many hours of hearing and spreading the day's topics and gossip, the visitors emerged into the bright light of day to wander back along the Sacred Road to either their homes or their places of business.

Fig. 21. Roman Baths on the Sacred Way.

I sought confirmation that the Baths which we see today would have been adapted from an earlier bathing facility during the period when Emperor Trajan was renovating the Sacred Way in 100-101 CE, as the general opinion was that it would have been. The most ambitious and powerful of the Roman Emperors always sought to stamp their mark by always commissioning the biggest and the best building projects to ingratiate the people, a not so subtle political manoeuvre, and Trajan was particularly adept when it came to that centre of all Roman activity; the Baths. Personally, I don't believe that Trajan could have resisted such a statement. Whilst as the Baths' entrance is approached through a gateway and pathway

Fig. 22. Roman Baths on the Sacred Way.

leading from this later segment of the Sacred Way it would appear logical to deduce they are indeed contemporary. The confirmation I received from Germany was that the Baths were indeed dated to the 2nd century CE, therefore possibly indicating Trajan. Though we must remember that the vast Faustina Baths (with Sudatorium) at Miletus were also built in the 2nd century and Faustina was the wife of Emperor Marcus Aurelius (121-180 CE). Therefore, at this point, all is conjecture.

Fig. 23. Roman Baths on the Sacred Way.

During the excavations, wonderful mosaic flooring was unearthed in the Baths which was dated to the 5th century CE. This naturally indicates that the high-quality status of the Baths was being maintained deep into the Christian period. The emphasis of religion may have shifted, but the Roman/Byzantine way of secular life continued to live and breathe, and, indeed, bathe. The best preserved of the mosaic flooring is to be found in the Apodyterium, or changing area, though they were to be found decorating the entire archaeological site in its heyday. As I mentioned above, the archaeology had been completed by the time I came to live in Didim; therefore I did not get to see these mosaics. Though upon the archaeologists' information boards they have reprinted two photographs; one depicting an attractive geometric design, the other a rather dramatic representation of a leaping dog, presumably a hunting dog as the canine is set in a schematic, and rather denuded, landscape and is framed by an extremely elegant foliage-type design. These have, of course, been re-interred safely deep within the earth and way beneath the trampling of forlorn sheep which roam the area today, as I look on equally forlornly whilst thinking, "Lucky is he who calls himself a sheep"! Though these mosaics would not have been seen for a particularly long period as the evidence unearthed by the archaeologists suggests that the Baths were no longer operational during the following century. Surely, that points clearly to the probability that the site, now of the Christian dogma, became far less populated as the Temple lost the significance it once so proudly boasted during its half-millennium of status and glory.

Revealing the Theatre

I recall the moment with absolute clarity. I was sitting in a friend's restaurant adjacent to the Temple when one of the archaeologists we knew came walking along the road, still dodging the heavy traffic in those days, with the broadest smile etched upon his face. "We have found the Theatre!" he exclaimed.

I visited early the following morning at 7 o'clock so as to miss the blistering heat of the August day, and 2011 was an especially hot one. I had not known the archaeologists for long at that particular time and thus felt it somewhat impertinent to start taking photos of their discovery, much to my chagrin now. Though I was shown around with an excellent explanation of the pertinent points of the structure; the front row seating in the auditorium, the stairwells leading from the 'vomitorium' (entrance and exit points) and the approximate size and capacity of the theatre.

The theatre has, in line with archaeological practice, been re-interred for its protection from the natural elements and, more cuttingly, unscrupulous human elements. Therefore a brief written sketch to help your imagination is certainly in order. One can discern the natural slope of a hill a little to the south of the present day perimeter of the Temple wall, just after an establishment called the 'Oracle Pansion', along the same alignment as the Temple. Though the archaeologists did have permission to excavate this area, which whilst still standing waste is 'privately' owned, they relayed later during the 'dig' the news that the Turkish Department of Antiquities had informed them that they would no longer be allowed to excavate upon any private land in the vicinity of the Temple. The theatre's size is similar to that found at Priene

Fig. 24. Ancient theatre during the excavations.

today, therefore holding in the region of probably 5000 spectators. From a spectator viewpoint it faced in the direction of Poseidon Point on the coast, where the Altar of Poseidon is located, which would have enabled the sea breezes to aid an acoustic ingredient to assist the projection of the actor's/recitalist's voice, with the added benefit of helping to cool the spectators. These orientations towards a helpful breeze were a usual part of the design plan for theatres, especially near the sea and in mountainous locations. I have always felt that to be a quite ingenious and deceptively simple idea, but then are not all the best ideas. Most certainly the theatre would have put on plays at various times, though the main feature at the Festival of Apollo (Didymeia) would have been oratory and poetic competitions, sometimes with the added accompaniment of music. Oratory, of course, was an intrinsic element of active political life and no doubt many an aspiring politician would test and hone this skill in front of a live audience on such an occasion as the festival. Make a name there and carry home a prize or two, well, one's career is firmly launched.

Though the presence of a theatre at Didyma was not always the case, for there is written evidence that some of these productions

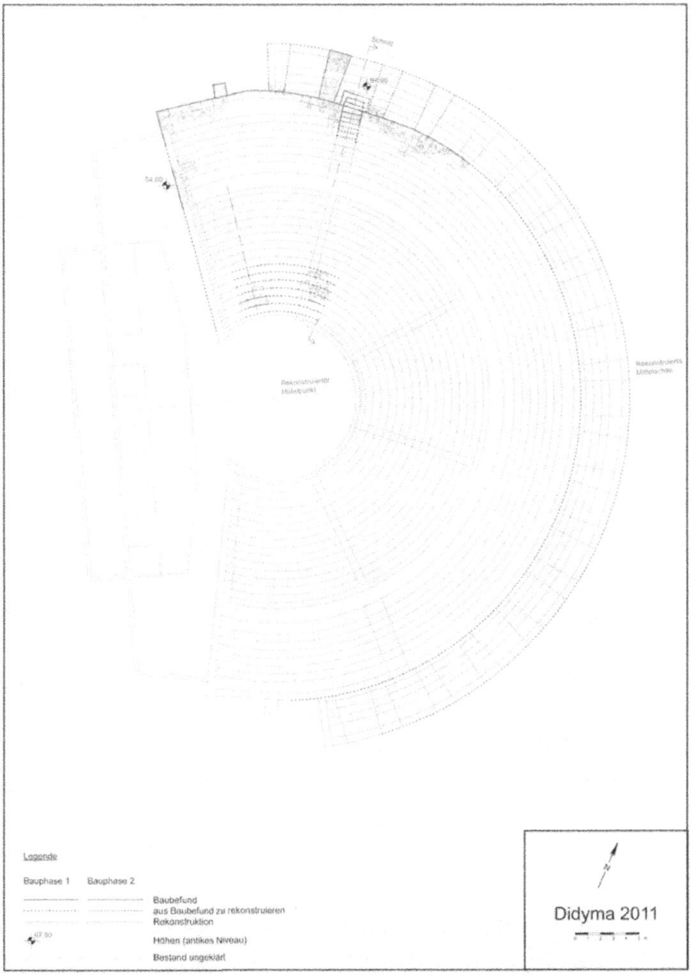

Fig. 25. Didyma theatre, preliminary reconstruction by M.Kohnert, J.Breder, H.Birk, A.Stöcklein 2011.

were performed at the vast theatre at Miletus, at least in the early period. Why construct another theatre when there is already an impressive and vast one available? Simply hold these parts of the festival at Miletus before the procession along the Sacred Way and save on a costly expenditure. This suggests to me that the Festival of Apollo at least at Didyma was probably of a shorter duration in the early years than what latterly followed. It may also have something to do with the piousness of the early days being a little more conformed to back then. This obviously alludes to there not being a theatre at Didyma at all for some considerable length of time. Whilst as the theatre discovered at Didyma has been dated, provisionally, to the second half of the 1st century CE it is entirely feasible that the transference of the events to Didyma took place only during the Roman era; that is after the last king of Pergamon, Attalus III, bequeathed his territory to Rome on his death in 133 BCE. The Romans began to reorganise the former kingdom in 129 BCE. We need to do much more archaeology to clearly identify that being the case, which cannot be forthcoming with the present restrictions imposed. The initial archaeology rather refutes this dominant Roman influence, in that the orchestra has been mapped as being of a circular design and not the semi-circle blueprint so often preferred by the Roman model. Therefore the theatre is undoubtedly Greek, which indicates that Rome did not meddle in affairs of local religion and recreation. Religion was one thing they positively delighted in adopting for their own selves. If, indeed, the dating of the 1st century CE is accurate, and I have been reassured that it is, then the explanation could simply be that of the gradual transference of cultural influence was being absorbed by the Ionians, whilst some architectural influences were similarly being absorbed in the reverse direction. In short, we need to have access to investigate more thoroughly. The archaeology pursued in 2011 did not uncover the entire theatre site, but enough was mapped to define the characteristics. The lower seating area consisted of 14 rows in three sections, fed by four stairwells, whereas the upper tiers comprised of nine rows in seven sections with access from six stairways. The orchestra is circular, as I mentioned, approximately 14 metres in diameter and the skene (stage building) spreads beyond this diameter in the usual manner. Therefore, it is a small theatre in the classical Greek style.

There is no doubt that a religious procession from Miletus to Didyma had always occurred from the instigation of the original site of Apollo's sacred grove and spring at Didyma, almost certainly from before the Ionian colonisation. The Ionian Greeks, as the Romans were later to do also, embraced the Anatolian rituals surrounding Apulunas, Hellenised the god's name to become Apollo and from the 8th century BCE immersed themselves in the very same cult, indeed, exported it back to the homeland which eventually became the Greece of this day. In typical human fashion, these religious rites were slowly evolved to embrace embellishments which made them all the more alluring to the intellectually expanding population.

A mystery waiting to speak

The Byzantine Chapel and Hellenistic foundations

This site is located just behind the Medusa Butik Otel on the south-east side of the Temple. Its discovery, in 2015, was the result of an inspired piece of archaeological detective work by the Director of Excavations of the German team.

The steady growth of the new religion of Christianity within the Roman Empire slowly presented what came to be perceived as a grave danger to the stability of maintaining the status quo; politically rather than religiously, for the Roman ruling elite had treated the superstitions of belief with contempt, certainly ever since Julius Caesar. To quote Lucius Annaeus Seneca (c. 5 BCE – 65 CE). 'Religion is regarded by the common people as true, by the wise as false, and by the rulers as useful.'

The Christians were, to Romans, initially a strange and clandestine group, one amongst many others that were tolerated as they constituted absolutely no threat to Roman values. It was only when Nero used the sect as the scapegoat for the fire which ravaged Rome in 64 CE that the quaint and lightly humorous view of the Christians changed, and a persecution resulted. In truth, very few of the sect actually suffered. Similar events occurred under the reign of Emperor Diocletian. The continuing rise in numbers of this new movement prompted Diocletian in 303 CE to unleash an Empire-wide persecution against the religious sect. This was given the validity of a 'blessing' from the pagan gods when the Temple of Apollo here in Didyma gave forth this edict.

Nevertheless, the Christians continued to find and nurture new

Fig. 26. Excavations of the Byzantine Chapel and Hellenistic Foundations.

converts and their numbers swelled. This inexorable growth culminated when Constantine was proclaimed Emperor by his troops at York, in northern Britain, during 306 CE, and after his subsequent victory over the other claimant for that title, Maxentius, at the Battle of Milvian Bridge outside of Rome in 312, he surprisingly declined to honour the gods for his success. It was only later that he claimed to be riding into battle under the protection of the Christian god, after purportedly witnessing the vision of a gleaming cross within the sky (probably the phenomenon commonly known as 'sun dogs'). Far from declaring Christianity as the exclusive 'religion of the state', Constantine demanded adherence to religious tolerance throughout the Empire; a politically astute decision which did, in fact, lead to Christianity becoming the dominant ideology in emerging Byzantium. Such tolerance was not adhered to, and pagans were subjected to murder and torture, their religious statues smashed. On a human level this is entirely understandable, for it is the barbaric urge of revenge after

Fig. 27. Excavations of the Byzantine Chapel and Hellenistic Foundations.

the persecutions they and their forefathers had suffered, and imaginably enflamed further by exaggerated tales of Christian torment, which incidentally also befell upon other peoples not of Christian faith; thrown to the lions in the Flavian Amphitheatre etc.

A rather substantial cessation to the emergence of this fledgeling religion occurred during 361-363 with the succession of Julian (Jovian) to Emperor. He was later given the soubriquet 'the Apostate'. Julian saw himself as a philosopher-emperor; he was indeed highly educated and desired to bring back the old pagan gods to the fore. Though rather than banish the Christian faith he allowed it to pull itself apart, using the unresolved issues of theology that were never entirely settled at the First Ecumenical Council of Nicaea in 325. Thus paganism began to see a new dawn. The priests of the Temple of Apollo, who had long complained of encroachment onto the sacred enclave by Christian places of worship would have seized upon this moment to severely damage or even raze this chapel to the ground during this period of pagan insurgence. The emperor

Fig. 28. Excavations of the Byzantine Chapel and Hellenistic Foundations.

succeeding Julian, Valens, was an Arian Christian who concentrated upon persecuting the Catholics, including the Catholic Bishops brought in by Julian to foment theological dissent, whilst leaving the pagans pretty much to their own devices. Though what was to follow in the shape of Theodosius assuming control of the Eastern Roman Empire, after the death of Valens at the hands of the Visigoths at the Battle of Adrianople in 378, was the death knell of the old pagan religion. Theodosius suppressed both the pagans and Arian Christians with equal verve and vigour, establishing the doctrine of the Council of Nicaea as the mandate for Christian Orthodoxy and cementing this with the Council of Constantinople in 381. The complete prohibition on any form of worship to the pagan gods meant that their demise was assuredly, if somewhat painfully long, sealed.

Fig. 29. Excavations of the Byzantine Chapel and Hellenistic Foundations.

We find here in the shape of a Byzantine Chapel, named 'Hagia Georgios' and measuring 11m x 5.5m, the whole of this story compressed into one modest structure. The chapel, when excavated, possesses an elegant apse of quality construction, sturdy foundation walls and some flagstones from the original flooring. Though what really interested me was the doorway into the building; this was the most obvious indication of destruction followed by a less

Fig. 30. Head of Emperor Constantine I, part of a colossal statue, now in Musei Capitolini in Rome.

skilled renovation. The doorstep, when unearthed, consisted of what looked suspiciously like a lintel and, inexplicitly, a small column capital; certainly not architectural features one would normally locate upon the floor and something of a shoddy piece of reconstruction. I can imagine the 'human, all too human' events unfolding. It may have initially been prompted by the pagan's annoyance of Christian encroachment upon Apollo's sanctified precinct, or, as I mentioned in the earlier chapter, the head priest or prophet imposing his own preferences and then claiming them to be the divine utterances of the god himself. It is my conjecture that the Byzantine Chapel, intruding upon Apollo's precinct, would have been damaged, if not entirely destroyed, during Julian's brief tenure. Alternatively, it could also have been as a result of something as prosaic as an earthquake, but that would remove much of the vibrant colour from this period in our human past. Whatever may have transpired, the pagans invoked their recovered power to persecute these 'bothersome' Christians. It should be no surprise to us living in today's world that passions raised by religion can result in the horror of pure unadulterated hatred. A mere fifteen years later as Theodosius came to power proclaiming a severe Christian ethic, all those that had been cruelly mistreated were frothing at the mouth for vengeance. Held in check, to some extent, by Constantine's politically astute proclamation of tolerance for so long, their seething had to lay dormant somewhat, even if the Christians were in effect immune from any punishment. But this hatred festered and was passed on through the generations. The brief sovereignty of the philosopher emperor Julian and his desire to reinstate the pagan values into society must have made the Christian's blood boil. It was likely that Julian was murdered by one of his own soldiers, of the Christian faith, on return from a military campaign against the Sassanid Persians. Either way, Theodosius' later decree prohibiting pagan practices unleashed the destruction of much of the prestigious pagan symbols here in Didyma. What gems we have lost to this blight of fundamentalism. Nevertheless, this particular site gives a fascinating insight to the tumultuous upheavals occurring when Christianity began to impose itself upon the entrenched pagan belief system and a way of life which rolls back into the depths of pre-history.

The Hellenistic or Roman foundations which reside beneath the chapel are a vastly larger area of high quality and precise foundations which attest to it being a structure of some significant importance; precisely why the Christians built a place of their worship above. The archaeologists have confirmed that it doesn't conform to any temple plan. Therefore as to what structure could be resting here, high upon a natural hill overlooking and aligned upon the same northeast direction as the Temple of Apollo, will just have to remain within our imaginations until another 'dig' is forthcoming. And in some ways that isn't such an awful position to be within. To have the trepidation and excitement of knowing that something is there and shall be revealed in due time leaves us waiting, pregnant with anticipation. I shall surmise what this structure could have been in the following chapter.

A curious alienation

The Hellenistic foundations

I believed that during the 2017 digging season the archaeologists would have been curious to determine the full extent, and purpose of the Hellenistic foundations which lay beneath the Byzantine Chapel. I have already noted that these mysterious stones are aligned along the same axis as the Temple of Apollo; a curiously non-conformist North-East facing direction. The norms for ancient places of worship generally adhere to an East facing façade, from where the sun would ascend.

A fascinating theory that I've heard has postulated that the odd positioning could be inherent in Didyma's name. As I have mentioned previously, 'didyma' means 'twin' in ancient Greek (the lingua franca of that majestic epoch), though we must be careful here as prior to the Greek settlement upon these shores, during the 8th century BCE, this area was decidedly Carian, the indigenous people. According to ancient mythology, Apollo and Artemis were twins, in Greek tradition from the bonding of Zeus and Leto, though certainly dating much further back into Anatolian prehistory where they were closely entwined with the Anatolian Mother Goddess, Cybele; when Apollo was known as Apulunas. In Carian 'didyma' had an entirely different hue of meaning; it derived from Mount Dindymus, whose location is, needless to say at such a far removed timeframe, ambiguous; whilst many epithets to the various places of worship was that of Dindymene. Though leaving the provenance of the name momentarily aside, I do not believe it to be too impertinent to imagine that by the time of the

Archaic temple, and most certainly the later Hellenistic delight we view today, the name 'Didyma' would be construed as meaning 'twin' or 'twins'. Therefore, why should this name influence the peculiar North-East orientation?

It could be conceived that this 'twin' symbolism held a heavy significance the more that time passed, for 'belief' is associated with an adapted tradition. The theory related to me adds more of this 'belief- based' cause and effect. This theory was presented by Hans Waltenberg and Wolfgang Gleissberg in their paper, 'Das Rätsel von Didyma und seine astronomische Lösung'. They postulated that the North-East orientation of the Temple, and this as yet not understood the Hellenistic structure, faced that way to point to the constellation of Gemini. For those of you that follow that dubious assumption that human lives are controlled by the stars will be very aware that Gemini's symbol is the 'twins' because Gemini in Latin means 'twins'. The Romans even gave the names of two of their most illustrious mythological figures, Castor and Pollux, to the two brightest stars in that constellation. Castor and Pollux, by the way, were twins.

However, astrology is merely another 'belief', without any credence of the evidence of empirical observation. It is delusional, though that is also what the ancients possessed in their supernatural imaginings. It is certainly an interesting theory as to why the Temple has its unusual orientation, but definitely not conclusive. We need to find evidence, for that is, and will always be, the only tangible proof.

Referring once more to the ancient inscriptions found on site, the evidence is well attested that the building of votive statues and, more importantly, monumental structures were a feature around the Temple. One, naturally, would not expect any remaining glimpse of such a, what would have been a magnificently grand, structure lingering on this site. The natural occurrence of the 'shaking earth' could well have been proved culpable, as it was for so much of humankind's hubris in the face of nature. It really is little wonder that those vulnerable beings invoked the wrath of some 'higher' powers to reason away their anguished tribulations.

Though such utter destruction which leaves no substantiation of what could have resided upon this foundation, measuring approximately 12 square meters, high upon the hill, inclines me to think that this total disappearance could only be attributed to that most vain and precociously vindictive species: humankind. The pagan belief preference being displayed would surely be anathema to the newly enshrined 'variation on a theme' rising in the deluded breasts of the terminally manipulated. Monuments and statues to the transient foibles of those who seek to persuade other souls to some grandiose illusion of their beneficence generally fall asunder in the most violent of ways. We watch it upon our TV screens with alarming regularity. I would not presume to guess what or who was represented, though the absolute and efficient annihilation of that which once stood here suggests a kind of frenzy that only religion can release.

Whilst that 'curious orientation' alongside the axis of the Temple, staring at some area within the heavens, continues to pull me back into that world of pure imagination; there must be a significant connection between the two structures. Isn't it just wonderful not to have all the answers? One is then free to mingle with all the ghosts from our ancient past and to consider them in an enlightened perspective, outside of any human-formed ideology. As the incomparable Douglas Adams of 'Hitchhiker's Guide to the Galaxy' fame once said, "Isn't it enough to see that the garden is beautiful without having to believe that there are fairies at the bottom of it too?" It would decidedly be yet another luminous 'feather in their cap' if the German archaeologists could shed some significant light onto this curious direction. Though perhaps we do need and require some mystery to haunt our subconsciousness. I personally enjoy viewing the Temple within that aura of the unknown. Whilst, in that case, a curious alienation is infinitely preferable.

A Temple that whispers from our past

The Temple of Artemis?

Ever since first visiting Didim in 1996 it has always struck me as absurd that a Temple of such crowning magnificence could ever be imagined to be standing so poignantly alone. In the Greek and Roman world, a temple sanctuary would abound with other smaller temples, treasuries, numerous altars to various gods and a whole plethora of statues, both votive and civic, dedicated to the gods and the 'great and the good' of humankind. Though modern Didim appeared content to merely convene on this one, extraordinarily majestic, structure and then to surround it with the trappings and atrocities of mass tourism.

Though in the recesses of the academic libraries of German, French and British institutions the initial findings of travellers, surveyors and archaeologists, dating from Ciriaco de' Pizzicolli's, aka Cyriacus di Ancona, visit to the Temple in 1446 and continuing into the early part of the 20th century, silently reside. Somnolently collecting dust they awaited an earthly resurrection. Excavations in the vicinity of the Temple were nigh on dormant from the period of the First World War, the Turkish War of Independence and throughout the Second World War. It was only during 1962 that excavations commenced, stutteringly, once more under the supervision of the German Institute of Archaeology, initially upon the Sacred Road, though now expanded across the entire site. They brought with them more sophisticated techniques and a more academic way of working; methodical, scrupulous to detail, and to outside observers, a painfully slow method. Slow it may seem,

Fig. 31. Excavated fragments of the building that could be the Temple of Artemis.

but they, and we, are now reaping the rewards.

I was fortunate to be on site when, in August 2013, the tantalising evidence of the foundations of a substantial wall were painstakingly unearthed in the garden of the present day mosque. Time, regrettably, was fast diminishing for that season's dig and so these fascinating stones were re-interred into the depths of the earth. All the archaeologists could be drawn on was that it was a wall of some description, though I sensed that many imaginations were working overtime, mine included. Needless to say that the following year's dig would seek some answers on this structure; thus in 2014 work focused upon this site and, in the space of a few days the corners were plotted. Meticulously the inner foundations of the structure were carefully charted, and it soon became apparent that the building conformed to a temple layout. The euphoria was close to tangible.

Fragments from the articulation of the building evidenced that it was a temple of the Ionic order, while finds of some Doric ar-

Fig. 32. Excavated fragments of the building that could be the Temple of Artemis.

ticulation retrieved nearby were probably from a Stoa (a shaded promenade and public meeting place) located in this vicinity. The proportions of the sections of the temple are mathematically harmonious; all revolving around the figure of 3.32m. The length of the entrance section is 2 x 3.32m, the central section 4 x 3.32m and the inner sanctum 3 x 3.32m; a total length of 29.88 metres. Whilst the width is 3 x 3.2m; total 9.96 metres. Therefore, given the thickness of the walls, the temple measures 30.98 metres by 11.05 metres. Its geography resides approximately two metres north from the present day mosque (actually the archaeology continues beneath the surface into the old Greek church/Turkish mosque, if this is part of the temple or another building is still a question of debate) and crosses the garden and a wall into the disused school grounds, beneath the dilapidated and vandalized building and into the playground to the west.

Though I named the site the 'Temple of Artemis?' in the subheading, thus far there is absolutely no hard evidence that this

Fig. 33. Excavated fragments of the building that could be the Temple of Artemis.

temple was dedicated to Apollo's twin sister. That is merely a poetically licensed conjecture of my imagination, though some of the senior archaeologists who have worked on the site share my 'gut feeling' and my sentiments. The dating was initially considered to be a construction of the 1st century CE, but has recently been

Fig. 34. West wall of the Adyton, inner sanctum of the Temple of Apollo, where delicate plans can be seen.

pushed back some 300 years to the possibility of the 2nd century BCE. The best line of reasoning leading to the conclusion that the temple behind the mosque was dedicated to Artemis is the correspondence between the drawing of the gable, or pediment, in the Adyton of Apollo's Temple with the width of the foundation behind the mosque. Moreover, the foundation is exactly three times longer than the width; proportion precisely 1:3 like the cella of the temple of Apollo. Interestingly, there is no parallel in the whole ancient world that people copied a model of a temple, enlarged it and built it. This process fits perfectly to the twins of Apollo and Artemis.

One piece of evidence from the early German excavations of the Temple of Apollo during the beginning of the 20th century revealed a photograph of a particularly well-dressed gentleman standing against the west wall of the Adyton (inner sanctum), inscribed upon the photo are series of lines; why? I questioned one of the archaeologists for a reason for this, and the answer astounded me. I had known for some time that some drawings had been found lightly inscribed upon the walls of the Adyton. They

Fig. 35. Well-dressed gentleman in front of the west wall of the Adyton of the Temple of Apollo.

were investigated in 1980 by Lother Haselberg. He found that the stylus used to make them penetrated mere half a millimetre deep into the marble, and realised that they depicted architectural plans used in the construction of various elements of the Temple. Haselberg noted that these plans were depicted horizontally and some perpendicularly. The general overview was that the horizontal drawings were on a scale of 1 to 1, whereas the perpendicular ones are on 1 to 6 scale. These drawings, which can only be viewed under certain lighting conditions, are extremely difficult to see, especially when one doesn't know where to look. Therefore, what is the well-dressed gentleman in the photograph standing in front of? Well, we can see it is a triangular composition and the only thing of a triangular design within a temple would be its pediment. But the Temple of Apollo, never being finished, at any time possessed a pediment. Also it is a horizontal drawing, hence a scale of 1 to 1, and then this depiction of a pediment is far too small to span the width of the Temple of Apollo. We are left with a mystery on our hands. Until, that is, the finding and measuring of the second temple, the 'Temple of Artemis'. It must have been a 'eureka' moment when it was realised that the inscribed drawing upon the Adyton's walls perfectly matched the width of this newly found temple. The drawing was produced upon one structure for an entirely separate one. Evidence enough to predict that the smaller second temple was of a later construction date than of Apollo's Temple, and that it was almost certainly completed with a pediment firmly in place.

Fig. 36. Former Orthodox church and now the mosque, where the building that could be the Temple of Artemis was excavated in the courtyard.

As for the demise and destruction of the 'Temple of Artemis' that surely must have occurred after Theodosius' edict to outlaw any form of Pagan worship. The Temple was either razed to the ground by the marauding vengeful Christians or simply converted into a Christian place of worship. It seems that the Temple of Apollo's mighty immensity proved too great an undertaking to fulfil such callous sabotage. If destroyed, then a church was likely positioned over the second temple's site, as a puerile declaration of total usurpation. This, in turn, was destroyed, maybe by an earthquake, and its stones used to build a new church in the middle

Fig. 37. Former Orthodox church and now the mosque, where the building that could be the Temple of Artemis was excavated in the courtyard.

Fig. 38. Excavated fragments of the building that could be the Temple of Artemis.

of the 19th century, an inscribed stone near an exterior stairwell around the back denotes "1830". Ironically this Christian place of worship has been usurped itself, and now houses the present day mosque whilst still overlooking the site of the pagan 'Temple of Artemis'.

Nonetheless, this is further evidence, along with all the other finds surrounding the Temple of Apollo, which indicates conclusively what an extensive centre of activity the whole vicinity once presented. I continue to see in my mind's eye a veritable metropolis.

Artemis' wishing well

Whilst observing the excavation within the schoolyard at the back of the mosque throughout the 2017 digging season, I thought that the archaeologists had found the clue that would have revealed that the 'new' temple was actually dedicated to Apollo's twin sister, Artemis.

Their trench was approaching a depth of 2.5 metres when another stone structure was encountered. The labourers jumped out, and the archaeologists dived in, to slowly peel back the last layers of earth. Gradually a circular structure began to emerge from the depths of time itself. The centre of the circular structure was vacant of any human laid stone. Surely, it must be a well. Though is it the well mentioned in an ancient script? An inscription upon stone and dated to the 2nd century BCE is extant, and tells of a well in proximity to the temple dedicated to Artemis, and inferred the possibility that the well also consisted of a golden statue adorning the structure. Its translation can be found in the Fontenrose's book along its the Greek transcription.

"Come with clean hands to the revered house of Naiads (springhouse) before the house of the virgin goddess and draw this holy flowing water, since Diodorus Olympos' son, minister of Artemis Pythie, placed me here".

[Ἁγναῖς] Ναϊάδων σεμνὸν παλάμαισι μ[ολόντες]
[δῶμα π]ρὸ παρθενίου τοῦδε δόμοιο [θεῆ]ς
[νᾶμα] ἀρύσασθε τόδε ἁγνὸν ἐπεὶ Διόδωρος Ὀλύμπου
σ[τῆ]σέ με Πυθείης Ἀρτέμιδος πρόπολος.[2]

Naturally, there is no sign of any golden statue any longer, not to my knowledge at least, though could this be the well? Of course, one's natural feelings are to convince oneself that it is, but wishing doesn't contain evidence.

As I knew that the 'vow of silence' taken by the archaeologists this year, due to sensitive circumstances outside of their control, would prevent me gaining any information there, I decided to retire to my library to delve into some research. Joseph Fontenrose's epic opus, though a little dated, was the first to be consulted; "Didyma. Apollo's Oracle, Cult, and Companions", a veritable authority for anyone studying the Temple of Apollo. I quickly grabbed the book and frantically leafed through the index to locate the pages concerning the Hydrophors of Artemis Pythie, and then read rapidly. A 'hydrophor' was the priestess who took water (from the well?). The inscription is also quoted. I then pondered over the maps I have of this temple to locate precisely where the well was in relation to the building. It was then that my euphoria plummeted.

Fig. 39. Excavations in the yard of a ruined school building.

The well is in the wrong position. It should be in front, or near, the entrance, but the positioning is to the back. That simply couldn't be correct. Unless, of course, the temple faced west, not east. Unusual, though not impossible, for the Temple of Artemis at Ephesus also has a west-facing entrance. The original architects could have considered that into their design. The two buildings were almost certainly contemporary. If, indeed, the temple does face west then the altar should also be located in the schoolyard. The altar was always to the front of any temple. Also, is this well flush to the temple's foundations, or slightly under? That is a difficult one to call, as it is so close as to be a matter of opinion. Obviously, if it is under, then the well must be older. The construction of the stonework appears rather rough-hewn, and nothing like the elegance found on the extremely fine masonry adorning the Hellenistic well in front of Apollo's Temple. In fact, this newly discovered well is so similar to so much construction throughout many centuries that it is impossible, for me, to date. Or, is it even a well at all? There are numerous examples of pits dug around temples into which were placed the votive offerings to the gods. The Greeks called them 'bothroi'. This in itself would be an interesting and quite seductive find, though not, alas, the historical revelation I was anticipating.

As always, a find always appears to throw up more questions than it solves. In my opinion, I believe this is probably not the well mentioned in the ancient inscription. I'll be the first to say that I don't know, but the evidence appears to be pointing that way.

These finds though do throw up questions which can lead to yet more interesting ideas and conclusions. For instance, there is an old German archaeological map displayed at today's entrance to the Temple of Apollo, I recall seeing it before meeting the archaeologists in 2011. This map portrays an area, next to the Roman Baths, which indicates that the area was considered to be the 'Sanctuary of Artemis'; presumably on the strength of the number of wells and fountains unearthed there and, I would think, on the evidence of the ancient inscription quoted above. We can still

Fig. 40. Artemis' wishing well, possibly.

see the depressions in the ground today showing the location of many basins, as well as some Roman wells. These were worked into the rock of the ridge which runs to the west of the Sacred Way. They obviously show a particular significance of the use of water in this area. Hence it was thought that there must be a link to the Hydrophors of Artemis Pythie. The site was also dated to be extremely ancient on the basis of some buildings which were excavated, which indicated that they were restored or replaced either at the end of the 7th century or early in the 6th century BCE. Though once the 'new' temple was discovered this notion had to be re-evaluated. It is no longer considered to be the sanctuary of the goddess.

I have just heard from my contacts in Germany that it has been declared that the find is, indeed, a well, though it has not been possible to come to a conclusion on when it was initially created. This confirms my impression of the rather roughly built mode of construction which was used consistently over a long period. My mind is now thinking that the 'well' may have been sunk in the Christian era after the pagan temple was usurped by the new religion, alongside a newly erected place of worship for their beliefs.

Fig. 41. Hellenistic well in front of the Temple of Apollo.

Once more the desperate need for a thorough archaeological excavation of the entire site surrounding Apollo's Temple arises. Trying to string a hotchpotch of individual excavations together in an attempt to glean a comprehensible whole is proving to be utterly frustrating. The trenches being sunk are no more than test holes, where any significant finds are chanced upon by the most amazing luck. As this particular site sits upon the ruins of an old disused school, frequented only by teenage glue sniffers of an evening, I am perplexed that permission has not been forthcoming to allow the archaeologists to excavate all of this area. The school buildings are in the process of being pulled down anyway by the local council, therefore why not let the professional and trained eyes do that work to investigate if any potential history is to be found there which shall be of immense benefit to the town of Didim. I'm sorry, but this bureaucracy invokes such a 'rant'.

A confusion of aims

As I continued lonely and silent walk in August of 2017, amongst the diligent, but unspeaking, archaeologists burrowing deep within the earth, it all rather struck me as being so familiar. For they were digging in the very same places as they were two years past; north of the mosque and the Byzantine/Hellenistic site behind the Medusa Otel.

Certainly, I had been excited by the finds of antique Doric and Ionic architecture in the foundations of the church/mosque, though I would have expected to find precisely those fragments precisely there. There is, in the schoolyard, a well, which if it can be corroborated to an extant 2nd century BCE inscription could confirm that the temple just north of the mosque was dedicated to 'Artemis'. Though as you read earlier this has now proved to be an erroneous piece of evidence infringing upon our understanding of this temple. These things happen. That apart, it has, all in all, been rather flat and uninspiring. Yes, it is pleasant to see old stone friends once more, but the same conversation becomes a little wearisome.

To give the archaeologists the benefit of the doubt, perhaps they were merely familiarising themselves once more to the site after their absence the previous year. Now, if they were to be addressing the question of what the square Hellenistic platform was utilised for, I would be intrigued. The papers have been published from the previous excavation, therefore, we know exactly what is there, so the work should, in my humble opinion, be making a comparison with other square based contemporary structures; and there are many in nearby Miletus, the city which administered the

Fig. 42. Neighbourhood of the Temple of Apollo.

Fig. 43. Neighbourhood of the Temple of Apollo.

Temple of Apollo and its environment. Given the location, upon a hill overlooking the Temple, I am inclined to imagine that its significance would have been highly regarded by its contemporary society. For these are foundations of some considerable weight. Of the site to the north of the mosque, apart from the interesting well, it is obviously the Doric Stoa they have been searching for, though the rather light weight of the foundation stones there casts a serious doubt if they could ever support such a structure. The map produced by the Dilettanti Society of London in 1812 depicts an 'Ancient Wall' located a little further to the north of their current excavation. I realise that this map is nowhere near as accurate as the maps produced using global satellite positioning, but it certainly would be worth investigating. It has proved to be rather inopportune that the ruling about not excavating on private land was issued a number of years past, for by my reckoning this places the location in the vicinity of yet some more inhabited shanty homes. I was told in the distant past that these houses within the old village were the subject of an agreement between the defeated Greeks and the newly emerged Republic of Turkey to preserve these buildings for posterity, in the anticipated event that cordial relations should return at a future date. We do indeed play host to a dwindling number of visitors from Greece whose distant relatives once lived in the village. There is also a small building in the Medusa Butik Otel which is dedicated to the friendship between Turks and Greeks; it displays many photographs from the days before the exchange of populations during 1923-24 and has a genealogy book in which one can trace the names, and thus the abodes, of those who once lived in the old village, which was then called Yorun. Evidently many Greeks visit to find the old dwelling places of their grand or great-grandparents. Personally, I never witnessed any. Therefore I can fully understand the sensibilities involved, though I must question if this is actually of greater importance than unearthing the environment around the Temple. You will no doubt guess my answer. Either way, I would still be inclined to take a quick scurry around where I believe this ancient wall is to be located, just to see if anything catches my eye.

Fig. 44. Neighbourhood of the Temple of Apollo.

I retired to a quiet café to quench my thirst and to ponder upon such mysteries. As I did I idly glanced at the archaeological map to remind me of previous years when exciting finds were springing up just about everywhere they put a spade into the ground. Yes, the vast size of the entire archaeological site makes a mockery of Didim marketing the area as consisting solely of the Temple. Certainly, the Temple is the hub of an elegantly designed circle which radiates out from that centre to all these places of immense importance in the town planning of ancient Greece and Rome. Though that circle remains incomplete to the northeast and the southwest. There is nothing there today except dereliction and people living in abject squalor. Surely, it must be glaringly obvious that there must be an abundance of archaeology of the highest importance upon the hill facing the main façade of the Temple. If I were a member of the distinguished dignitaries of the Milesian elite, or the Roman Governor of Asia Minor, or, possibly, even the Roman Emperor himself, where would I place my Apollon villa? Of course, one would position such a grand statement as a sumptuously designed villa directly facing the magnificent façade. Absolutely no archaeology, to my knowledge, has ever been pursued in this area, neither has any permission been given for it to do so.

One would think that a jewel such as this site would be the focal point of tourism, alongside the intense professional interest of academicians. The Temple remains eerily quiet as merely 32,000 visitors pay to enter Apollo's Temple annually. Meanwhile, an estimated visitor number in Didim is 400,000 each tourist season, according to Didim Council. That number is plainly woeful. The latest attendances figures I have for Greece's equivalent attraction, the archaeological site of Delphi, numbered a little shy 140,000 visitors, and that has probably increased as the Greek economy has decreased. Delphi, of course, has long been set upon the tourist agenda; it has been extensively excavated, it has an on-site museum, a whole plethora of literature to fill the historical appetites of its guests and is widely advertised to people visiting the country. One simply cannot miss it.

As for Didim, well, the reading is going to be hurtful to the local population. I have attempted to explain without getting too political or personal, but a thorough clearing of the archaeological site has been, and continues to be, beset with that old human failing of abject greed, both financially and geographically, which manifests itself politically in local decision making. Apart from the few but excellent information boards set up within the Temple and along the, forever closed, Sacred Way there is no other information available, the tour guide books being sold at the entrance kiosk are 25 years out of date, whilst most disgustingly of all is that the major tour companies in Didim do not promote the Temple at all. I have been told that there are some minor tour companies, hidden away within the backstreets that do conduct a guided tour of the Temple. Though that does not negate the apathy shown by the larger and prominent agencies who prefer to advertise the more

Fig. 45. Neighbourhood of the Temple of Apollo.

lucrative deals of overnight stays at Turtle Beach in Dalyan and at the stunningly picturesque wonder of Pamukkale, as well as the day tours to Ephesus where one spends more time in carpet, leather and onyx shops than actually at the glory of this magnificent city. I recently quipped to a Turkish tour agent that his slogan should be, "Come to Didim, and we will show you somewhere else"! He didn't laugh, merely squirmed with embarrassment. In every hotel foyer, moneymaking tours invade the guest's eyes, though none reveal the existence of a temple only a short dolmuş (local bus) ride away. I have lost count of how many times over the years I have spoken to visitors and asked if they have been to the Temple. Many have simply never heard of it.

I have tried asking these people why they do not promote this superlative Temple, and I suggest that you also try too whenever, as I hope, you decide to visit Didim. If you ever receive a reply I am sure that you would find it as cringingly insular, and in a moribund state of conservative inertia, as I.

Hidden background of the Archaeologists work

It was immensely gratifying to welcome back the archaeologists from the Martin Luther University of Halle during 2017. We certainly missed them the previous year, when regrettably they were not given the permission to excavate on the dates that would have coincided with the University's summer semester. I certainly hoped that they could make up for that lamentable lost time by succeeding to astonish us all with yet more evidence of Didyma's ancient past.

Fig. 46. Access road to the Temple of Apollo.

Though it must be remembered that there are many facets of the profession, their endeavours are not restricted only to rolling back the pages of the past. A most crucial function of their responsibilities also requires the 'site management' stratagems of maintaining the Temple and its environment. For without that tender caring we would eventually have precious little to investigate, whilst tourist numbers would immediately drop if the site were to prove too dangerous a place to enter. In their absence this important feature was neglected the previous year and walking around the site, as I do so frequently, it was obviously beginning to show the tell-tale signs of such inattention. For instance, it was on the archaeologist's recommendation, if not insistence, that the road passing the Temple should be closed to all traffic, bar the emergency services. Needless to say, no one heeds the signposts at both ends of the road; motorcycles of all description tear through there with a shameful recklessness, whilst if the barriers are down or the access point next to the mosque open, then cars, delivery lorries and tractors pulling their load have no qualms nor care about the damage they are cumulatively causing.

Actually, I believe that the archaeologists missed a trick on the road management front, for even if the people were a little more mature and adhered to the traffic regulations, many locals continue to use the track which winds itself along the southern border of the Temple; past Oracle Pansion. That, confusingly, remains a through-road. Certainly, the Pansion and the houses there require access, though placing some bollards around halfway down would prevent lazy drivers and lazy minds from destroying the Temple from this angle also. Aydin Municipality, that is charged with the responsibility for the implementation of road restrictions around the Temple, fulfilled their requested obligations admirably, though I believe that having either a police or, probably more attainable, a zabita (council police) officer present should be enough to further curtail this absent-minded vandalism upon both roads. As I have often said, "Logic was born on the other side of the Aegean".

Moving inside of the Apollo's sanctuary, the area designated as the tourist site, once we've paid our entrance fee, one can observe the fragility of much that requires constant supervision. The

Fig. 47. Metal supports set in concrete preventing the "Oracle Pansion" tumbling into the Temple's precinct.

first thing I noticed was that the recently installed wooden stairs descending into the site are warping and splitting due to the unending battering they receive from our summer sun. I noticed especially elderly visitors and young children gingerly negotiating their way down this precarious flight of splinter-ridden stairs. Surely a lick of varnish, off-season, should prevail for the duration of the summer influx of visitors. It was only towards the end of the tourist season when I finally observed that this stairwell was taped off to the public, directing them onto a less hazard-strewn path into the Temple precinct.

The retaining boundary wall has always been of concern to me, as each passing year, it appears to be sloping ever further inwards as if it is ready to tumble down at any moment. The opportunist drivers, certainly of the heavy vehicles that pass illegally, regrettably have no concern for either the Temple or to the people strolling along taking in the breathtaking scenario unfolding before their eyes. Such a callous disregard from drivers, unfortunately, is part

Fig. 48. State of the perimeter wall built by Wiegand in 1906.

Fig. 49. Erosion occurring at the perimeter wall.

and parcel of life in Didim in general and this discourtesy continues into this haven of tranquillity away from the brash and boisterous mayhem of the holiday resort.

Fig. 50. View over the Stadium track and the southern stylobate from the repaired perimeter wall.

The archaeologists went to great length to support the wall, below the café viewing area of the Oracle Pansion, with a heavy-duty casing of iron girders bedded into massive concrete blocks. That establishment would have surely tumbled into Apollo's precinct by now if it were not for the German's sterling work. This is purely conjecture, though I was under the direct impression that the request to close the road passing the Temple was to prevent this eventuality occurring along the rest of the perimeter walls, or possibly this request has fallen foul of the famously duplicitous language used here. I have heard the wailing cries of café and shop owners bemoaning the perceived loss of trade which they have incurred. But I have sat in one of the many quiet cafés on innumerable occasions and noticed that at least 90% of traffic consists merely of those passing through. Rarely does anyone stop.

Fig. 51. German archaeologists undertaking repair work on the perimeter wall in 2017.

We really should be ensuring the integrity of these walls. Evidently, this original wall was constructed at the time of the early excavations around the Apollo's Temple in 1906, also by a German archaeological team. It had certainly stood the test of time, 113 years, surviving numerous earthquakes, including the 'big' one in 1956 which left the old Greek village in the state of dilapidation we continue to witness today. Today's excellent archaeological team reorganised the stones to place the larger ones securing the base of the wall and the lighter of the stones at the pinnacle; thus enabling it to further endure the rigours of time.

Whilst inside the sanctuary there is always a constant flurry of activity whenever the archaeologists are here in town. I have witnessed ingenious lightweight heavy lifting contraptions reorganising the fallen masonry in the vicinity of the Temple. One such of these clearances which they constructed three years past was

Fig. 52. Repair work on the southeastern perimeter wall in 2017.

used as the alternative entrance when the wooden stairs splintered and warped. Scaffolding, each 'digging season', hugs the standing and broken columns and the walls of the Pronaos as repair work continues apace. The concrete supports, which are inspected every year, of the standing antique columns of the Temple would crumble and disintegrate if they are not replaced or refreshed, they also need to be saturated with water throughout the blistering months to prevent them from being worse than useless. Along the Sacred Way this activity is also in evidence, as a specialised team gets to work to identify and resolve any problems they may encounter. Not forgetting the placement of the recently erected excellent information boards, so as we (whenever we may be once more allowed) can enjoy and understand this spectacular site.

Understandably the archaeological finds shall always dominate the headlines, garner the prestige and capture the imagination, though we require this solid foundation work within which to appreciate the glittering discoveries emerging from their earthen graves. Whilst this may also be the time to applaud the Turkish labourers who 'break their backs' in the sweat-inducing heat; for it is they who wield the pickaxes and shovels, get the dirt upon their hands and blister in the incessant, unforgiving sun.

Thus, these actions do, indeed, remedy many of the 'disaster' situations which could confront the entire archaeological area; the one and only focal point of intellectual interest in Didim.

The covenant of Apollo

A link to our very origins

The belief in a religious system is generally driven by the all too human need to seek comfort from a particular deity or deities, especially in the case of ascertaining an 'explanation of misfortune'. Arguably that is the sole attraction of this illogical supernatural occupation. Nevertheless, there is a strong emotional need to make sense of unexplainable events. It is this state of being within the dominion of the 'unknowable' which prompts fantastical notions of cause and effect. Our everyday superstitions of childhood stories melt away once we attain a level of education to elevate us from this simplistic mode of thinking. Though those larger questions which generally articulate themselves along the lines of, to paraphrase Paul Gauguin, "Where do we come from? What are we? Where are we going?" are too abstract to find a simple singular answer. Hence, the gods continue to live in this dank and dour corner of people's minds; swirling mysteriously in the ether. Thus, it has always been.

We have touched upon the rituals surrounding the pronouncements of the Oracle at Didyma and we probably all imaginatively pictured a scene where shadows loomed deep. I know of no evidence to support a nocturnal meeting with the god, but I believe that the knowledge of theatricality would not have been lost on ancient civilisations. Imagine the half-light of flickering torches, the lyre and the sombre wind instruments coiling upon the faint breeze and the ethereal sound of the accompanying choir resonating within the walls of the Pronaos. Drama and mystical belief

Fig. 53. Overlooking the Adyton from atop of the "labyrinth" passage way. Note the thickness of the walls.

entwining to set the imagination aflame, a sense of inhabiting a higher unworldly realm enveloping all who were gathered within those sanctified marble walls. And not only was Apollo manifestly present, but all the other gods too. If one needed reminding then merely glance into Apollo's great precinct to see the, "encirclement with altars and statues of every god" (W. Günther, 1971, from Robin Lane Fox's 'Pagan & Christians').

During the excavation season of 2013 I was kindly escorted by an archaeologist friend to venture inside the locked gateways of the Cresmographeion and into the 'labyrinth' climbing to the summit of the Temple. Firstly, it was hardly a labyrinth having merely one turn of a stairwell, but onward I climbed those deep steps. I recall thinking that these people must have had muscles in their legs the size of tree trunks. As soon as we reached the top I was afforded a unique view over and above the Temple; to my left the open air Adyton, directly below me the Cresmographeion which would have been roofed in antiquity, whilst to my right, an eagle's view

Fig. 54. Looking down into the Pronaos from the top of the front façade.

over the Pronaos, which would have also been covered by a roof. My archaeologist friend pointed out that they were beginning to think that, possibly, there would have been a religious beacon, atop of this roof, burning brightly into the night sky attracting the attention and awe of the congregated people gathered within Didyma. A symbol denoting the important high-status event occurring, much in the same way the beacon burns brightly during our Olympic Games today. My first thought was "Zoroastrianism", the ancient religion of the Persians and their one sole god, 'Ahura Mazda'; no, a single god wasn't purely an original Jewish belief. Within Zoroastrian belief fire possessed the ability to purify and was the ultimate symbol of spirituality. That thought dispersed to be replaced by the wonderfully famous Greek myth of Prometheus stealing the fire of the gods on Mount Olympus to give to humankind, and how he had to endlessly suffer for that deed. Whilst if we are thinking of the greatest giver of light and heat then we are in the correct location, for one of Apollo's many

Fig. 55. A bird's-eye view over the Adyton from the height of the labyrinth.

accoutrements rang out his praise as the 'god of the sun'. Though this is now questionable as to its correctness, for the epithet was thought to have derived from 'Lykeios', from the stem being 'luc', as in Latin 'lux'. This 5th century BCE linguistic origin of Anatolian explanation and of his and his mother's Lydian epithet, 'lada', earth, were later proved incorrect by French excavations in Lydian Xanthus during the late 20th century. Nothing ever goes in a straight line in this line of work!

Fig. 56. The high steps of the "labyrinth".

Nonetheless, it is a feature of many, if not all, religions that fire is a dominant element in their belief systems. Is this yet another echo

Fig. 57. Meander design of the labyrinth's ceiling.

from our primaeval past? One from where we were still roaming the savannahs of Africa? From a reverberation deep within our DNA, of a time when our only source of the fire was from an occasional lightning strike or a gas pocket ignited by some natural occurrence, it was here where a human change became entrenched. These groups, I shall not call them 'tribes' for they probably never numbered enough, would have attempted to keep a flame alight, even if only it were smouldering kindling, for that would enable them to warm themselves and deter predatory beasts during the chill savannah nights. Inevitably one emerged who was proficient in maintaining the flame, and this became his/her dedicated role within the group whilst the others went off to forage. Here, in the 'keeper of the flame,' we have the very first religious leader. Everything led on from that one moment, the hierarchy of social order and an organised system of shared belief stemmed from a prosaic duty which became a necessity.

The attendees at the Didymaion would have had utterly no understanding of the endless link to the grasslands of Africa, it did not matter, but they would need scant reminding, according to the understanding of contemporary believers, that Apollo was well versed in delineating the predilections of all the other gods, whilst eminently capable in articulating his own preferences. This attribute made the Apollo deity particularly attractive to the populace for this made him more accessible than some of the aloof and vain of the religious pantheon. We may even have here an echo of the idea of one uncomplicated god emerging from the mayhem of a crowded Mount Olympus, which could explain the comfortable internal ease of future Christianity. It possessed an air of familiarity. Constantine's alleged esteem of the one god doctrine of Christianity would have had a familiar sound to the many that used Apollo as an intercessor with the supernatural sphere.

The belief in Apollo filled this function admirably, especially at the times of plague which struck ancient Anatolia with frightening regularity. It was a sign of appreciation to pay lavish honour upon him in the forms of sacrifice and song, be aware of him at all times so as to ensure his swift interception of any future ills; yes, it was a superstitious belief which appealed to each and every individual that 'they' would be spared misfortune. Such belief in Apollo's powers resided deep within the origins of his cult, at least to the Greek and Roman population, where he was said to have intervened to exonerate an outbreak of plague in Miletus

Fig. 58. The solitary unfluted column from the roof of the front façade.

by reciting an enigmatic alphabetic hymn. Another of his accoutrements was that of the god of music, for which this conquest of the plague with the power of song obviously attested to. If all this feels somewhat similar to the beliefs that some people hold close to their bosom to this day, then I suggest that has more to do with

Fig. 59. View of the Cresmographeion from from atop the "labyrinth".

the simple yet complex procedures of evolution, coming from a common root, than any so-called divine revelation.

When the earth convulses

The recent 6.3 magnitude earthquake during July 2017 was a stark reminder of the power of nature's forces. It was also a sharp indication of why humankind has always felt the need to invent supernatural deities that would protect their fragile existence in the face of such awe-inspiring forces... all to no avail, naturally.

Taking pride of place upon Didim's beachfront is located a modern statue, alluding to being bronze, of Poseidon the Greek god of the sea. Though Poseidon was also known in antiquity as, 'the earth-shaker', the bringer of earthquakes, thus people were careful to pay due deference to this particular god. The people of antiquity, of course, knew nothing of 'plate tectonics', which were only postulated and then confirmed during the 1960's. Therefore for humankind to explain and 'know' they, as always, referred these events to the will or displeasure of a figment of their clouded imaginations. Though the ancient's perception of equating a shaking earth with the god of the sea was, not surprisingly given their empirical observation of nature since the time of Thales of Miletus, accurate. Most tectonic plates rest under the coastal waters of continents, seas and oceans the world over.

Pausanius recounted that the origins of a previous temple, or a number of temples, may have dated back to the 2nd millennium BCE, though they must have been of modest construction, possibly wood, as no evidence has been conclusively attested. What we can attest is there had been two previous temples to Apollo at Didyma, the first a late-geometric period construction started at the end of 8th century BCE, the second a late-archaic temple dating to the 6th century BCE. Both probably would have encoun-

Fig. 60. Modern statue of Poseidon on Didim's beachfront.

tered some distress from the ever-threatening earthquakes, though the Archaic Temple escaped the natural catastrophe of destruction by the 'earth-shaker', only to fall foul to human misfortune when the Persians looted and smashed the Temple before razing it to the ground with fire, after the Battle of Lade in 494 BCE.

As an additional note, it was during the archaic period that an altar to Poseidon was erected close to the lighthouse of Didyma, I believe near to what was called 'Poseidon Point'. I fear that we may lose this archaeology forever for it could, in future, be buried under the concrete and glass of yet another vacuous all-inclusive 5-star hotel.

Fig. 61. Fallen columns at the back of the Temple of Apollo.

Recovery was not possible under Persian rule. Though when Alexander the Great invaded and completely routed the Persians, the Archaic Temple was followed by the construction of the Hellenistic Temple. This probably did not occur earlier than 331 BCE, as Alexander levied a punitive tax against the Milesians for their part in defence of the city in conjunction with the Persian Satrapy. Seleucus, one of Alexander's generals, in control of the east following the demise of Alexander, returned the cult statue of Apollo, crafted by the legendary sculptor Kanachus of Sicyon, to the Temple after it was taken to Ecbatana, the Persian summer capital, after their sacking of the Archaic temple.

When the rebuilding of the Hellenistic Temple finally commenced, it too suffered from periodic visitations from 'the earth-shaker'. Quite obviously, a unified whole will be stronger than a partially built structure, a point which periodically affected the construction, as earthquakes continued to undo the labour, sweat and toil of the engineers and stone masons. The Temple was still not quite complete some 600 years later. Slowly at first and then apace after the edict of Theodosius abolished any form of pagan worship, the venerable old religion slunk into the shadows and annals of history. A church was placed within the inner sanctum; whist the Temple's marble was quarried and burned to produce lime mortar.

An Italian traveller and humanist, Ciriaco di Filippo Pizzicolli, also known as Cyriacus di Ancona, (1391-1452), reported that he saw the Temple still standing during his visit in 1446. What he probably saw was the columns of the peristyle, whilst the columns in the Pronaos and Cresmographeion were severely damaged due to a fire in the 10th century when the area was being used as a storage facility. Merely the lower portions of these columns, fortunately, survived as they were covered by a mixture of earth and rubble, one can still view them today, whilst the higher segments were metamorphosed into lime and ash. Ciriaco was the first of a select few of European visitors to Didyma before 1800. It was soon reported that the Temple had been significantly demolished in an earthquake of 1493. For an earthquake to destroy so much of the Temple it must have been of a far greater amplitude than July's 6.3 magnitude. Two surveys by the Dilettanti Society of London between 1764/5 and 1812 reported that, "the temple appears to have been thrown down by an earthquake", as the columns are aligned in a common direction.

The 'earth-shaker' was never to rest, of course, and the shattering and splintering of the landscape continued, and continues. Though one which is within living memory and still recounted by the elderly inhabitants of Didim is the earthquake of 1956. For this we have accurate records. The epicentre was just south of the Greek island of Amorgos in the south Aegean where a mammoth 7.7 magnitude was recorded (that is 14 times the strength of the latest July quake). It occurred on Monday 9th July of that year at 06:11. Though the power of the magnitude would have decreased somewhat by the time it hit the old Greek village, then called 'Hisar' in Turkish, surrounding the Temple, the quake, nonetheless, flattened almost all of the buildings situated there. The Temple stood unmoved. Such destruction caused the government of the Republic of Turkey to build a new settlement, called Yenihisar, which is now the centre and heartbeat of the modern town of Didim.

Fig. 62. Buildings damaged by an earthquake in Didim.

In the archaeological world it was hoped that a full excavation of the environment of the Temple could now proceed, as happened at Delphi. Though the crumbled remains of the old village were soon re-occupied; by those who could not adapt to modern high-rise living away from the land that they farmed, and those who merely wandered in to set up unofficial homes within the debris. They are still there today, 61 years on, and growingly supplemented by part-time holiday homes, which obliterate the grand scale and design of the environment around the Temple. I believe vehemently that here in Didim we have an archaeological site that is every bit as important as the famed oracle upon the Greek mainland, possibly not larger, though who knows until the archaeologists are free to excavate?

Projection of imagination

I continue to read of archaeological finds from all over Turkey being reported by the national press, in some considerable depth, though little or nothing of Didyma. I am not disputing that these reported finds have been mightily impressive; they have been, though they hold no more significance than the finds which the archaeologists have uncovered here in Didim over the past decade or more. Especially when taken as a whole. The German team have been meticulous and methodical in their approach to the entire site, and have creatively peeled back so many layers that it is clear to see that the whole area was once a vibrant and living town. Though only the Temple of Apollo peeks through the millennia to see the light of this new day, they have unearthed a wealth of finds upon which we can draw detailed inferences to our collective human past.

Even with all this evidence, as I clearly illustrated upon a map I produced in 2016, the people who de facto 'rule' and influence the direction of this town have persistently ignored this pertinent information. I am sorry, though it appears plain to conclude that the 'closed shop' which controls this town has no vision outside of their own short-sighted interests. I have heard calls from all quarters, for over a decade, calling for Didim to improve on its image of a vain hedonistic holiday town, frequented by rather poorly educated visitors. Didim could be so much more than that, for we have a fine cache of educated people residing herein already. It is true to state that there is only so much that councillors can hope to achieve, as the burden to effect change is ultimately firmly in the domain of the Department of Antiquities. Trying to contact these people appears to be an impossible task for an outsider, even though I have been a resident within Didim since 2003. I have been warmly received at the British Museum, conversed leisurely with the on-site archaeologists from the University of Halle, but have heard not as much as a groan from any local politician let alone one from the Antiquities Department in Ankara. I find that most disconcerting. Naturally, I appreciate that this department has a considerable workload, especially when one realises that the entire Republic of Turkey is one vast museum. This truly was the crossroads of the world, and the evidence is there to support that notion in abundance. I certainly do not desire to distance them by being too belligerent; that shall serve no purpose to anyone.

Fig. 63. Monumental gateway or tetrapylon in Aphrodisias.

I should not linger on those things that have not, and never will, happen, though precedents have been set with regards to the adaptation of human habitats that have overlain important historical and archaeological sites. Naturally, as the Temple of Apollo and its surrounding environment is the only intellectual centre of attraction of this town (by no stretch of the flightiest imagination

Fig. 64. Stadium in Aphrodisias.

could anyone hope to call the beachfront and its accompanying activities intellectual) the Temple must be pivotal in bringing about this change; though it shall require people possessing vision, a stubborn resolve and a strength to make controversial decisions.

Two key examples immediately spring to mind when considering the Temple and its impressive environment, the first is Delphi on mainland Greece and the second is Aphrodisias not far from Nazilli here in Turkey.

During the excavations in Delphi, by a French team of archaeologists in 1892, the village which stood atop of the ever-enlarging site was moved 1km to the west to facilitate the uncovering of the rich culture of Classical Greece. It was, after all, the fabled 'Centre of the World' and the most important oracular shrine of the entire ancient world. Didyma is acknowledged as being second in importance and therefore the most paramount venue for receiving the wisdom of Apollo in Asia Minor. No doubt the motivation for the village inhabitants was their newly found patriotism after their secession from the Ottoman Empire after 350 years. Whilst the excavations of the accidentally found city of Aphrodisias were a decidedly Turkish affair, albeit sponsored by the dollars of an

Fig. 65. Reconstructed Treasury of Athens in Delphi, built to commemorate their victory at the Battle of Marathon.

American-based Turk and his sponsors. Fortuitously stumbled upon during 1958 by photographer Ara Güler as he was returning home after a photo shoot in nearby Denizli, he became lost and ended up in the tiny village of Geyre. Once in this begotten and forgotten backwater he was intrigued to find remnants of classical architecture proliferating the village's buildings and strewn within the surrounding fields. Hastily recording these surprising finds photographically he sought to alert the authorities, but to no avail. The silence he received is a deafness I can attest to. Dismayed but unperturbed he decided to contact the eminent Turkish archaeological scholar, Kenan Erim working at the University of New York in the United States. Beguiled by Güler's story and photographs the professor travelled to Turkey, located the village, and soon realised that Güler had stumbled upon the ancient city of Aphrodisias, famed for its impeccable school of sculpture. Here the inhabitants of the village which lay on top of the ruins were persuaded and cajoled to remove their dwellings and mosque 2km from the archaeological site. The villagers' motivation there was probably the vast amounts of American Dollars flowing in.

Fig. 66. Ruins of the ancient Temple of Apollo in Delphi, overlooking the valley of Phocis.

Sixty years later, and still the cogs of bureaucracy continue to screech, groan and splutter their mournful tune of intransigence, resulting in the pitiful sight surrounding the Temple of Apollo. I am sure that every single tourist visiting the Temple cannot have failed to notice the squalor that people live within along its perimeter. This is hardly a gleaming picture of the country being portrayed to foreign eyes. They should really be re-housed, off-site, in better conditions and given land for their chickens and goats to wander. Personally, I would be happy to see the cafés and bars also moved off-site, though these are owned by the people I alluded to earlier and have a tentative link to history by being the descendants of the subsistence farmers who moved here during the exchange of populations between Greece and Turkey in 1924. Really, can 93 years be considered as history when it is sitting upon 3,000 years worth of accumulated accomplishments from previous civilisations?

Build in Light

I shall hope that you will indulge me in a flight of imagination stimulated by some recent correspondence I have received. I was sent via a friend in Norway some photographs of a model representing how the Temple of Apollo would have appeared as it neared as close as it ever got to completion; they are from a German publication entitled, 'Antike aktuell. Didyma und Milet im Modell' by Walter Voigtlander. I have been unable to contact anyone in a position to give me permission to reproduce these photographs. You may wish to seek for them yourself, though as to if the book is still in print I have no evidence. Therefore it may be worth searching for in cyberspace.

I have often dwelt upon how understated and underused this magnificent Temple, and its notable array of accompanying structures have been treated, almost neglected to little more than a backdrop to the commercial enterprise of wrestling cash from gullible tourists. The excavated areas of the Sacred Road and the Roman Baths have been imprisoned behind locked doors for more years than I care to recall, with eager tourist eyes peering through the prison's metal bars. I have lamented the fateful demise from being at the pinnacle of the prestigious cult of oracular contact with the weighty deity of Apollo; revered from before the Hittites, throughout the whole Greek sphere of influence, jealously attacked and plundered by the Persians and, finally, esteemed and sacrosanct to the most famous of Roman Emperors. A few Turkish friends have inquired of me over the years as to why the archaeologists do not rebuild the Temple. Of course, I hide my smile and try to explain to them that the Temple would no longer be a classical

Greco-Roman wonder to behold, but rather a 21st-century pastiche of a superb original. I always shy away from reconstruction. Even if we could imitate the methods of construction contained within the originals, we would invariably lose some of its mystery and magnificence, along with the ambience and pathos which an original exudes. 'Virtual simulation' is preferable for that can be upgraded to accommodate findings of later enquires. And we can obviously use all the new technology available to us in these exciting days, so why not build in light?

Though this would entail committing to an injection of considerable investment, I foresee that such an outlay would be recouped quickly with the amount of worldwide interest, free exposure to the many differing formats of today's news media coverage and a rapid rise in tourism as people flock to observe a unique attraction. As soon as I, open-mouthed, viewed these images of the model of the Temple it immediately struck me that here was an opportunity for this town to rebuild its image; one that catered for the History, Archaeology and Art market, which has always been successful in attracting overseas visitors from the entire globe.

I recalled the fantastic 'Sound and Light' shows I experienced at the Pyramids in Egypt, and my recent evening at the Theatre of Ephesus where I was magically transported by the simply stunning light show in the peerless production of Tchaikovsky's ballet, 'Romeo and Juliette'. Naturally, I pondered if that success could be replicated here. Could you imagine the splendour, as darkness began to descend, of a hologram gradually emerging in the thickening gloom, building its way from the stylobate (the surface on which the columns stand), slowly, to the pinnacle of the entablature? The visual wonder of seeing a representation of the Temple as it was as it neared completion would be awe-inspiring alone, whilst add to that the audio of a narrative, in different languages on differing nights, surely that would be something truly unique. And why stop at only Apollo's Temple? Why not introduce the other ancient structures that we know of; the Roman Baths, the shops and statues along the Sacred Road, the Temple of Artemis, the Stadium, the Theatre and the Byzantine Chapel, all bathed in glorifying light? Whilst when, rather than 'if', the archaeologists find more (for there certainly is much more) they too could be added in the future.

The visitors would surely arrive in droves to view this spectacle, though who has the vision and forethought to be brave enough to deliver such a stimulating enhancement to this town, so long entrenched in the sterile stench of conservative lethargy? Or possibly the project should be managed from Ankara under the auspices of the Ministry of Culture and Tourism. I am also sure that private sponsors would be more than willing to invest in something that would greatly augment Turkey's prestige worldwide. The ballet at Ephesus proves that the quality and technical abilities are present, and professional in abundance, to achieve a new dimension in bringing visitors to our shores.

It is high time that we returned the dignity to this most elegant Temple, restore its 19.71-metre columns in light to beguile our visitors, fling open the gates to the Sacred Road and release the entire site to further archaeological investigation. Now, who has the strength to carry the beacon?

I fully realise that such a proposal shall in all probability absolutely horrify the purists, though not all possess that sublime ability to conjure in their imaginations an awe-inspiring ancient structure from a few dour marble blocks strewn amongst a scene of desolation. The locals here in Didim scoff and raise their eyes while pronouncing, "Load of old stones", with a dismissive wave of their cigarette holding hand. To paint a picture in light would set free those imaginations residing within some dark and dank dungeon, without compromising the integrity of the original masterpiece. Whilst if the Temple, and the other buildings in this environment, are to have a value ascribed to them, then in bucolic minds that value must equate in terms of a financial guise.

Meeting at the Miletus Museum

There being many contradictory replies to my questions concerning regulations in place around the Temple prompted me to arrange a meeting with the curators at the Miletus Museum. As I walked the steps leading to the museum it struck me that I had never visited here since the revamp a few years ago, so I decided to have a cursory look around. I was most impressed with the design and layout, lighting, temperature and the content of the information boards, in Turkish and English. The artefacts displayed are softly illuminated and are ordered in a chronological format which provides a coherent narrative to the display.

Though as I knew that Miletus was once the most important, and richest, of the Ionian city-states, I was surprised that so little was displayed. Admittedly, in the courtyard there are a vast amount of statues and inscription stelae, though much of this was of mass-produced Roman era manufacture and not the high-quality high-status statuary which would have once adorned a city of such significant importance. Probably the more prestigious artefacts are to be located within other museums of Turkey and Europe, but Miletus is not the focal point of this book even though the Temple at Didyma could not have existed without this once imperious city. Nonetheless, I was still delighted that a fine result has been achieved at a small provincial museum, curiously missed by many upon the tourist trail.

Fully sated, I then proceeded to the meeting with two of the curators in the office section of the building and was warmly welcomed. As later they appeared a touch reticent in giving their names I do not feel I should relay that information. I am sure it was nothing sinister on their part. After the usual preamble, I began to introduce my questions. I was surprised that the area around the Temple was only designated as a 'Protected Status' in 1976, and has received two reviewed upgrades which have both increased this protected area, the last being as recent as 2015. Needless to say, I was buoyed and pleased at this news. Though my next question provoked a quick discussion between the two, 'What exactly is being protected'? I discerned that their reply was one of those formulaic answers designed to say nothing specific whilst including everything, 'All the stones above and below the ground are our cultural heritage'. I was beginning to feel I should have spoken to the stones.

I was to hear this answer to many of my follow up questions, though at least they confirmed that the ancient Greek and Roman architecture is included in the protected status. Which is sometimes rather less than discernible when I observe the way some areas are treated by the bucolic people of the village who occupy the site; though it is hardly their fault if they do not receive an education. Basically, they were saying that no archaeology could be undertaken to reveal the Greco-Roman period, for that would entail disturbing the stones of the collapsed village houses. My follow up to that somewhat evasive answer was quite simple.

'OK, fine, if that is the proscribed view then what about excavating the Theatre and the second Temple permanently? Neither of them has any description of architecture overlaying them'? (Well, actually the theatre does have some, but that could be worked around). That, I am afraid, left them somewhat perplexed, and I received no coherent reply. Obviously, this was becoming a tad more difficult for them than they had initially imagined.

Of course, I questioned them on the blatantly, 'in-full-view', illegality being conducted upon the renovations of many of the buildings in the area? Who was responsible for inspecting and maintaining them in the spirit of the 'Protected Status'? Alas, I was met with that inertia so familiar when dealing with bureaucracy anywhere in the world. Every reply sounded like a carte blanche

Fig. 67. River God statue from Faustina Baths in Miletus.

excuse for doing nothing. They were not so much in unison when I asked them the reason why the Sacred Way is not open to the public. The first response was to say that the archaeological survey was not yet complete and that the archaeologists themselves had asked to keep it off limits to the public.

I knew that was utter rubbish, for the archaeologists spoke to me quite specifically about this subject. Therefore I merely commented, 'That is curious. I wonder why the archaeologists erected those splendid information boards three years ago in readiness for the arrival of the public?' To which the other curator reacted with the explanation that actually there is no management in place at the present time as if that would refrain me from developing this line of inquiry any further. By this time I was too wearied by circular arguments even to be bothered to ask for any form of timescale when that shall happen. I knew I wasn't going to receive any type of answers of any substance and guessed that these curators were probably too junior to be asked these gravities of questions. I figured it was time for me to leave, and to leave them in peace.

I cannot say that I disliked these curators for they were kind enough to give their time and were extremely pleasant. They were probably not expecting such a grilling and no doubt, as I said, their hands were probably tied in giving a personal opinion. I think they realised that at the conclusion of our amiable chat, for when they asked I told them I am an art historian and gave them the relevant information of the publications I have written for various media outlets.

I shall attempt to contact a more senior person at a future date. I am only sorry that was not possible up to this point. Strange how it took me merely two e-mails to arrange an appointment with the Senior Curator for Greek and Roman Antiquities at the British Museum, but for some provincial museum, forgotten in the back of beyond, this has proved thus far to be unobtainable.

The Exchange of Populations House

I attended a meeting at the Didim Chamber of Commerce during 2014 where the members of Didim Council were taking a 'Question and Answer' audience with the foreigners residing within this town. My ears soon pricked up when someone mentioned the terrible state of the buildings surrounding the Temple of Apollo. I listened with keen anticipation to the Councillor's reply. Sadly it amounted to nothing more than the usual enigmatically unenlightened, 'We have plans for that area'. Equally as sad, if not more so, was my realisation that their intent was going to be solely based upon 'Tourism' and not, not ever, 'Culture'.

Yes, their diminished foresight transpired to go no further than instigating yet another pastiche of a Greek village, so profitable in other areas of this region to gullible tourists. But they were going to, hook or by crook, place this monstrosity slap bang in the middle of an archaeological site of immense importance. And one which is still under the process of investigation and excavation! Surely the Aydin branch of the Ministry of Culture would intervene at some point. Alas, that process of maintaining the integrity of the 'Protected Area' never surfaced.

Naturally, I did enquire during my meeting at Miletus Museum about the validity of such a scheme immediately after being told of this 'Protected Area', only to be told that Didim Municipality owns the two buildings which were under consideration and permission (from where?) was given for the go-ahead. Nonetheless, some news seeped through this silence that money had been obtained from the Ministry of Culture and Tourism to finance a museum here within Didim. Now, this sounded really promising,

Fig. 68. Exchange of Populations house.

for it is something which would culturally enhance the area enormously. Though neither of the two sites was initially stipulated it was assumed that this museum would be the large building which used to be a hospital in the days of ethnic Greek occupancy, the one which the archaeologists currently utilise as their finds storeroom; merely 'bric-a-brac' pieces of architrave and the like. The 'Depot' they call it.

That site, alas, was to prove too much of a financial burden to be viable. That was quite an acceptable reason which no one could take umbrage with. Therefore the other location owned by the Didim Municipality was chosen, smaller but sufficient. Up to now, all very logical, open and above any real criticism, fine. It is at this point where minds diverge. The house they had chosen lay atop the hill directly facing the main façade of the Temple, an area never before excavated. Now my rather naïve assumption that before the restoration of this house a substantial archaeological survey, and if necessary a test trench or two sunk, never even remotely manifested itself. It was a straight 'build on what we got, pull down the dodgy stuff and do it again'.

What an opportunity, a great opportunity, missed. We could have answered so many questions about this dominant hill directly in front of the main façade of one the most glorious Temples of antiquity still standing today. I felt as fallen as the many columns littering the ancient site this very day.

Work commenced during the early period of 2018. Sundays, the workmen's day off, saw me forever traipsing around by the renovated house which would become the Didim Museum, or rather the 'Exchange of Populations House'. A monument to the Treaty of Lausanne undertaken in 1923 to move the Muslim believing people of Greece to the newly formed Republic of Turkey and the Christian believing people from this new republic to the Greek mainland; or rather more accurately, Turkish speaking citizens to Turkey and Greek speakers in the opposite direction, irrelevant of religion.

This was, in all likelihood, due to the slaughter of civilians by soldiers of the opposing forces, at varying times. When soldiers are in 'kill mode' they take some calming. Maybe with exceptions, the civilians themselves appeared to be neighbourly close, weeping at the departure of their friends and longtime associates. This 'monument' is particularly relevant to the people of 'Hisar', this district of Didim where the Temple stands, for the original families, of whose descendants still reside amongst us, were transported here during this exchange.

Such were the humane and thoughtful qualities of Mustafa Kemal Atatürk and his fledgeling administration, the people who were placed here in Didim mainly came from the Kavala region of northern mainland Greece. Strangely enough not far from where, during the Roman period, the marble was sent from to build the Temple they awake to each morning today. I wonder if they know that. I doubt it, though it would be wonderful to think that this curious animism of rock empowered these early enforced migrants to find comfort here in a strange land.

Therefore this 'monument' to souls that have passed, with their

Fig. 69. Modern roof tiles for the Exchange of Populations house.

cursed capacity for suffering, arose into the promise of a 'museum' to these poor people's plight. I do not believe that anyone could deny them such a worthy accolade. Though I still insist that by ignoring the chance to excavate in this designated area for ancient remains is not justified by the familial homage to merely a few hundred people. Maybe you shall, or shall not agree. That privilege is yours. Or even both could have been realised if only one transient local politician possessed any inkling for history and not votes. I, therefore, classify this house of the 'Exchange of Populations' as being cultural, yes, though not with the same gravitas as the Greco-Roman site we could have (I believe, definitely have) beneath this area. And all they had to do was to dig a metre or two to establish, one way or another, the validity of this theory.

Those Sunday strolls around the periphery of the restoration area were giving me glimpses of what could have been. This house appeared to reside atop another building. It was initially difficult to discern due to the builder's work tools, general litter and rubble cluttering the site. Obviously, I took many photos. These I sent to my connections in Europe, and their reaction was to 'keep on looking, you may have something here'.

I had hopes of the walls I could see being of Byzantine construction, though I recalled the archaeologists telling me that on many occasions they had excavated a place of dwelling thinking the same ideas only to be disappointed when the evidence pointed to a late 18th to early 19th-century construction. When detritus of this site finally began to clear, I could plainly see that Byzantine was a hope which was three centuries adrift. At least I looked though, at least I did that.

Naturally, I continued to look at the finer points of the reconstruction as it was coming together. The words I had heard in the Museum came floating back into my mind about the rules and regulations concerning any building in this protected area ('All the stones above and below the ground are our cultural heritage'). These words were further enforced by the knowledge that I have known places pulled down because of illegality in contravening these regulations. Therefore, what were the council workers doing using modern day materials within a 'Protected Area'?

The ubiquitous concrete, used in just about every modern construction, was being employed atop the stone walls in readiness for the roof to be placed upon. I looked around and found the roof tiles, no surprise; they were of a modern design which I know are deeply frowned upon and again contrary to the proscribed regulations. Neither do they have the empathetic qualities required for a truthful rendition of a historic house. Something is awry, and silence has descended.

I fully realise that it is an honourable intention on the part of Didim Council to attract visitors to the vicinity of the Temple and its other major archaeological sites, though why do they not take heed that they do not know anything about a culture which existed here before them. That they appear not to have learnt anything at all about this archaeological site is the testament to their fallibility in distinguishing between Tourism and Culture. A fact echoed by the popular, but still monstrous, 'Vegan Festival' they stage each year upon the road which runs around the Temple.

It is regrettable that they do not do more to bring attention to the Greco-Roman site than put the twin columns upon their council logo and maintain splattering the over-used image of the Medusa head in the small amounts of literature I have seen produced. It seems that they cannot see beyond the next tourist bus, usually full of people who don't give a damn.

Pushing the territory of the 'faux pas'

Throughout 2018 the Ministry of Culture and Tourism here in Turkey was pushing for the return of ancient artefacts which have been stolen from this region of the world. A region with an impressive surfeit of wondrous treasures from a whole host of different peoples and cultures. One that echoes the sentiment that this particular region has been correctly, and enigmatically, described as the 'Crossroads of the World'. Some of these claims are justifiably obvious in their demands; they have been stolen by organised crime cartels for a hungry worldwide art market, no one is disputing that in the slightest. Though others are somewhat more complicated, and certainly no so clear-cut.

This latter scenario is certainly felt by some of the most prestigious museums upon this planet. Institutions where an appetite for acquiring knowledge from all corners of this sphere was transmitted to an eager audience, the general public. These institutions would also maintain that many, if not all, of these artefacts would not be with us today to even argue the point. Therefore eyes are upon countries, such as the Republic of Turkey, to ascertain if they can and do protect the ancient monuments which lie in situ. I am rather afraid that the situation here in Didim has not warranted such a favourable verdict. I shall explain them briefly.

As I espoused in earlier chapters the issues of the Sacred Way being forever closed to the public is an irritant, especially to long-haul travellers. I spoke to a lady who had journeyed from Beijing in China, she was most perturbed at not being able to walk the small paved area close to the Temple. Many more groan, I can assure you. The other point I raised was the re-opening of the modern road which passes the Temple. The archaeologists successfully argued that the heavy traffic that merely passes through was damaging the Temple and its environment. It was duly closed for one full year, even if the motorcyclists who could negotiate the barriers never took a blind bit of notice. Then the road slowly but surely began to be opened. At first, it was after certain times during the evenings, a favourite time for locals to attend the many cafés and bars. Later it increased throughout the day in a seemingly random fashion (but never when the archaeologists were in town). Whilst now, archaeologists or not, the road is once more fully opened and back to impressing the same cumulative damage it inflicted earlier. As one of the archaeologists, a Turk (as a new law states that at least 51% of persons on a dig must be Turkish citizens), said to me, 'It is a shame they have opened the road again'.

Asking a local friend, who was born in the Hisar village, she told me that it must have been upon UKOME's instructions. UKOME is the Turkish roads authority, made up prominently from politicians and people from the business world. She assumed that it would have been the Aydın branch, though upon researching I found that their Didim address was in our local Chamber of Commerce. Intriguing!?!?

Another rather faux pas moment occurred in early August, just before the archaeologists arrived for their annual excavations. Seemingly unbeknown to anyone in town the placement of tables and chairs and a heavy crane ushering in a grand piano over the broken columns were all placed into the Pronaos of the Temple. News spread quickly, and the local reporters were soon on the scene. It transpired to be a private dinner party for a large Turkish multinational company and their distinguished guests from abroad.

Even more surprising was that the company, Koç Holdings, input a lot of energy and money to promote archaeological projects. That permission for this metamorphosis from a temple to a grandiose café must have come from the highest levels of government, presumably in Ankara. Which certainly does nothing to alleviate the fears of the museums of Europe and the USA. A rather patronising and ill-thought folly to 'impress and flatter' their foreign customers. Whatever happened to the 'Protected Status' I had heard them so proudly exclaim to me at Miletus Museum?

There is also the small matter of taste to be addressed. I am fully in agreement that the ancient pagan religions of the Greeks and Romans have long been usurped by the present day variations on a theme. Though isn't it rather tactless to despoil a belief once so highly venerated by such illustrious peoples? A little empathy would not go amiss. I am also aware that the superb theatre at Ephesus is utilised to bring spectacular musical productions presented to the public. Yes, though that is within a setting designed for that form of entertainment, not a temple sacred to our ancestors.

Some people tried to make the pitiful suggestion that the festivals in and around the Temple could, and often would, become far more boisterous during the ancient festivities than a mere self-congratulatory dinner party. I replied to them all using the same words, 'We are simply the custodians of their history and should not attempt to emulate the ancient's actions. Thus allowing us to preserve those moments in time precisely. That is not too difficult to understand, is it?' Which is to say; that it was their activities, in their time, and in their religious place of worship for them to perform whatever brought them closer to that euphoria of religious frenzy. Not ours to decide their criteria and actions. Quite an easy dismissal for a historian.

Others passively, in 21st-century materialistic tone, murmured that if the event was staged to raise money for the upkeep of the Temple, then that would be fine. It wasn't, and no one has ever said so. Whilst as to Aydın Province's Director of Culture and Tourism, Murat Yilmaz's, comment that mats were placed under every chair (and the piano I assume) to protect the 'historical texture' is not witnessed by photographic evidence.

If there was some brief light upon this unfortunate incident, it was the realisation that many more people in this town really do care about the Temple and its environment that had never occurred to me previously. The professionals in this and related fields and the academicians I knew would contact me and applaud my corner, but so many ordinary people from Didim? That was a pleasing surprise.

The Spring of Apollo bursts forth

An aquatic dilemma

From high expectations, my dreams fell upon that bleak reality that archaeology does not always deliver the promises formulated within the imagination. I guess that is just the ground we are working on, where disappointments are required to savour that sweetness that comes with an exhilarating find. And to be fair, here in Didim the archaeologists have been unearthing those exhilarating finds in abundance over the past decade. Snippets of information can also be gleaned from an anti-climax, which adds breadth to the understanding of the site which is being conducted. To everyone's chagrin, the trench excavated alongside the second temple, behind the mosque, revealed merely that which it did last year; when a well or a bothros, a pit for votive offering to the gods, was discovered.

Another smaller well was uncovered next to the one which we all knew about, but it was rather like watching a fond old movie once too many times. It felt flat, uninspiring and rather laborious to view. If there was an upgrade to the history then it was solely to confirm that these were indeed conduits to allow access to the groundwater, and not votive offering pits (bothroi, the plural of bothros). Furthermore, it slowly became apparent that they were not contemporary to the foundations of the second temple (I never believed they were), being sunk long after that sophisticated structure.

It was rather an aquatic-themed itinerary which the archaeologists set themselves this year (2018), for their other main task was

Fig. 70. Inundated area next to the Apollo Temple.

to locate the source of the water which inundates the southeast corner of Apollo's Temple. Two trenches were opened along the road which passes the Temple. I spoke to the archaeologist in charge of this task at one of the trenches, a most affable and charming person. She was under the impression that this water leak had only caused a problem in the last year, though it had been occurring since 2016 when the archaeologists did not receive permission to work here.

Nonetheless, this water seeps through the ground, from whatever source, and emerges low down along the deep slope which descends to the foot of the southeast corner of the Temple. It is a veritable quagmire. Though I am aware that the Temple is built of sturdy construction, moving water is, after all, the greatest threat to any terrain, man-made or natural, with its ability to erode everything in its path. I cannot imagine that anyone would wish that to happen. For if this corner were to subside there would be a significant threat that the single column of the Temple may well follow the slump into the earth. Admittedly, that is neither imminent nor plausible with the amount of liquid we are speaking of here, though I would be better pleased if the reason for this sudden appearance of a swamp could be found and alleviated.

The pipes beneath the road appear to be in an adequate con-

Fig. 71. Inundated area next to the Apollo Temple.

dition, and the long-standing wells dug into the hill above the Temple have not been found to be the causation. Samples of the water have been sent for chemical analysis in the hope that this may pinpoint the source. Thus, we can but wait.

Fig. 72. Inundated area next to the Apollo Temple.

One of my concerns is that there were some well-holes sunk a couple of years ago on the permission of Aydın Council, I believe. I wonder if these may, now that they lie dormant of use after an outcry from local people, be to blame. Some groundwater may have been released and, as water does what it does, has found the easiest route of eroding escape. Another scenario which is equally as viable, and yet again human-made, could be the increasing number of new houses being built, or 'reconstructed' if one prefers to maintain the dominant ideology, in the surrounding 'Protected Area'. Water does not start flowing for any reason, and I am quite certain that the archaeologists shall ascertain the source of the problem.

I had spent many hours wandering around the site taking numerous photographs and obtaining measurements of the depth of the water. These were then relayed to my European contacts, which in turn were passed by them to specialists in the disciplines of geoarchaeology and hydrogeology. It wasn't long before I received an answer which set me aflame with imagination and sheer delight.

A cursory inspection of my photographs immediately revealed, to their trained eyes, a classic karst hydrogeological phenomenon which can, and often does, appear after an earthquake. Karst is formed from the dissolution of soluble rocks such as limestone, dolomite and gypsum; it is, therefore, prone to splintering under pressure and erodible by water. Forever, this rupturing earth.

The entire peninsula between Miletus and Didyma consists of this karst rock. Modern-day Didim, therefore, is in an area which is liable to be jolted by a fracturing of the tectonic plates at any time. Most are minor, which I believe caused a small amount of water to be released from its subterranean imprisonment into the southeast section of the precinct two years before. The fissure was opened at that time, whilst the 6.4 magnitude quake during July 2017 further expanded this weak point, thus enabling more water to gush forth into this same area.

It was confirmed that the foundations of the Temple itself are massive enough to withstand the incursion of this amount of water. I was assured that there is no threat to the Temple subsiding into this quagmire. However, there are a good number of architectural fragments which have been placed on this side of the Temple which require relocation to a dry area; these mainly include the remains of a Christian church that was erected after the demise of the ancient religion. This should not prove a too arduous a task, and I am sure that a plan has been implemented to enact just such an undertaking.

More worrying is the condition of the archaic terrace wall—temenos—which arches in a semi-circle in front of the main façade of the Temple. A section of this wall is directly in front of the path of the water; its foundations are not substantial enough to confront the undermining qualities of water erosion and, indeed, pressure. Obviously, the problem requires urgent attention, not least because, being from the Archaic Period, the wall predates the Temple by at least three centuries. It was in situ when the Persian soldiers plundered, smashed and then burnt the old temple to the ground in 494 BCE. If only stone could speak.

Even though this situation is serious and disturbing for those of us whom adore the Temple as one of the finest structures ever created by humankind, it has brought to light the fascinating complexities of geology which have shaped the Temple's destiny. It certainly gives the clearest of pictures of how the Oracle Spring of Apollo could simply appear, or disappear, as a result of an earthquake when the karst is shifted and fissured by nature's forces. The ancient population would not have known of these naturally occurring phenomena and would have taken it as a heavenly or earthly sign on the mood of the gods. It is oft quoted that the Sacred Spring dried up after the Temple was ransacked and destroyed in 494 BCE and that it only began to flow once more after Alexander the Great swept the Persians from this land. I think it is safe to say now that supernatural intervention was definitely not the cause; rather it was a geological event.

What a fortuitous time to be alive in ancient Didyma today to have seen the Sacred Spring gush into life once again. Shall we hear Apollo's voice echoing from the ancient stones, issuing forth his prophesies, in the deepest darkness of night? Surely, we are witnessing a rare event.

Or is this a rare event? I was speaking to an old friend of mine who grew up in the village surrounding the Temple, her great-grandfather was one of the migrants during the Exchange of Populations, and she recounted to me a story of her youth when she and her friends always referred to this very same section of the Archaic wall as the 'weeping wall'. She explained, 'It was always wet in that area during my childhood'.

Certainly, there is the the possibility that successive earthquakes have folded to close the water channel whilst other seismic quakes have split the karst allowing the liquid to flow once more. Plainly, this does not venture into the realms of the supernatural will of the gods.

As with the unanswered questions from the Miletus Museum, I have received no information from the archaeologists about any results from the sample of water taken for analysis, regardless of the numerous e-mails I have sent. For people engaged in a profession which the principle ethic should be of informing the public, there are serious issues that need urgent addressing. I am certainly not disputing their impeccable credentials, merely the lack of interaction with the public.

I have been reliably informed that their funding will be up for review by the German Archaeological Institute in 2021. I am certain that it is crucial for them to be allowed to continue by yet another 'event' during November of 2018.

Alerted to the swamp by the local populace, because it was 'beginning to stink', the water company sent in some pumps to remove the water. Heavy duty pumps, which quite possibly also carried away the smaller items of archaeological evidence. They really should have waited for the professionals to return before taking such drastic and damaging actions.

My reoccurring theme of ignorance and negligence never seems to subside.

A glimmer of light shines forth

During September 2018, the newly appointed Minister of Culture and Tourism, Mehmet Ersoy, published a rousing agenda of his hopes and desires for the future for this lucrative and important element of the Turkish economy. It was certainly impressive, though missed some glaring issues.

Obviously, the tried and trusted mantra of an 'extended tourist season' was yet again aired. No doubt that would have fallen on deaf ears within Didim. Why? Because so many are simply fatigued from putting in long working days, each and every day, they require their precious downtime to largely recuperate the energy they've expended.

Certain proposals were suggested which have always died a death at the embryonic stage of their brief existence; i.e. golf courses and 'other sporting scenes'. Didim has even tried a winter cinema season. Though to be honest the people resident here are just plainly pleased with some respite from the holiday hoards. Even the foreign residents within Didim breathe a sigh of relief in the knowledge that they shall not receive any more family or friends for another few months.

Though why, if Mr Ersoy wishes to encourage foreign people to Turkey's shores, does he not abandon the old ideas that have never, nor or ever likely, to work? Yes, Turkey does have absolutely fantastic beaches, enough sunny weather occasionally even enough in the coldest of months, though the sea part of the equation may well be out of bounds as the water temperature is far too cold to all but the most hardiest of souls. Those, to people with no imagination, are the three reasons why foreigners venture to this land.

I am thinking solely of Didim here, but it is equally applicable to the rest of Turkey. I am not alone in believing that a journey to another country consists of none of the above criteria. My motivation has always been cultural: history, art, architecture, literature, and music. You can keep the beach for all I care. Of course, I am stipulating that the culture should be 'high culture', not the 'pop' variety. I am a scant eater, though many people would be correct to add cuisine to that list. Turkey has one of the best cuisines in the world and so many local variations. It is a culinary delight, apparently!!!

That does not mean we have to deprive the less educated British visitors, the most numerous of the foreign influx each summer, of their English Breakfast, Sunday Roast or Fish and Chips, though please we don't have to have it so prominently invading the senses of those who are a little more discerning.

If one wishes to capture a better class of customer, then you must entice them with quality service in a quality environment. Though it seems that is far too much effort in Didim. As a café owner once said to me, 'The idiots get what the idiots want. Makes no difference to me as long as they are giving me money' He then added, 'I have to smile at these people, do you know that?' Yes, the Didim representatives run around Europe doing their promotional fairs, whilst their wives are doing some heavy-duty shopping, yet most people I know within Europe have never even heard of Didim. In Britain, this is not helped by the British tour companies who persistently call our town Altınkum, which is merely the beach area.

The none-too-subtle intent of this book is to bring attention to the exquisite Temple we have resting here, the hidden treasures of the magnificent environment which encircle this monument to humanity and the sumptuous and sometimes bloody history which underpins Didyma's past. Yes, outside of the Temple itself the place looks squalid; dilapidated buildings ready to fall at the next earthquake, tacky tourist souvenir shops and a road serving far too much traffic for a visitor to feel comfortable. Isn't it just ironic that the road that should be open, the Sacred Way, is closed and the road that should be closed, the damaging through road, remains obnoxiously and noisily open?

Yes, I like and enjoy the café/bars, though I do wonder about the legality of some. Whilst Mr Ersoy may well enquire about the new houses being built around the periphery of the village, a 'Protected Area', the owners of which have exploited a loophole in the amnesty law. This law grants amnesty for buildings built without a habitation certificate (i.e. illegally) before the 31st of December 2017, as long as a habitation certificate is applied for before the 31st of December 2018. These issues are generally of the mundane nature such as extending or closing a balcony, converting a roof space or a basement storage area into a living space.

Unfortunately, some unscrupulous people have built entire new properties upon the rubble-strewn land they own, passing it off as a renovation (a renovation of what?). They have also, surprise, surprise, been placed on the housing market and at extraordinary prices!!! This amnesty also casts a huge shadow of the validity of having this, or any, archaeological site designated as a 'Protected Area'. All protected areas within Turkey should be excluded from this amnesty, unless certain criteria were fulfilled, namely protecting the integrity of ancient structures which are threatened with too much intrusion of the commercial (greedy) elements of any society.

We have a most important focal point of the historical culture here within our midst, the knowledge that it is not Turkish, but Greco-Roman should not make any difference to a Minister charged with the Cultural Heritage of Turkey. That such human history and rich artefacts reside within the boundaries of this country make these objects the Ministry's responsibility. The obvious desire to 'repatriate' artefacts stolen from this land from foreign collections and/or museums is honourable, but one must make sure that those objects which you already have are lovingly cared for and protected from that financial wrath of an uneducated few.

As I alluded to earlier, 'We are the guardians of our collective past'. Protect it. I am anticipating that that heavy responsibility shall find shoulders broad enough to rest upon.

Photographic Appendices

These wonderful aged photographs and drawings dating from the early German Archaeological Expedition during 1906 under the directorship of Theodore Wiegand and some from the 1960's, judging by the clothing, have been added to my collection over a number of years by generous donations from various persons. Many of the cafés surrounding the Temple display enlarged versions of these images upon their walls, alongside others of which I have been unable to locate the originals. When studying these images, a number of points attracted my eye immediately; I was astounded at the amount of buildings which were removed to extradite the Temple from its rubble-strewn tomb and realised that the recovery of important history was obviously valued more highly then than the present. Whilst the photographs from 1962, and later, revealed that the condition of the houses within the village was in a considerably better state of appearance and repair than the eyesores which blight the scene today. One can only assume that the people who moved into these structures just after the earthquake of 1956 were not the original owners, and thus never possessed the love or care to maintain the houses respectfully. This particular point enforces my argument that these people should be re-housed off-site at a location which would be both legal and comfortably convenient to them and their families.

Fig. 73. Old photographs of Didyma.

Fig. 74. Old photographs of Didyma.

Fig. 75. Old photographs of Didyma.

Fig. 76. Old photographs of Didyma.

Fig. 77. Old photographs of Didyma.

Fig. 78. Old photographs of Didyma.

Fig. 79. Old photographs of Didyma.

Bibliography

- Joseph Eddy Fontenrose, 'Didyma. Apollo's Oracle, Cult, and Companions', University of California Press ,1988
- Dilettante Society of London, 'Antiquities of Ionia', Payne & Foss, Pall Mall; Longman &Co., Paternoster Row; Rodwell & Martin, Bond Street, 1821
- Robin Lane Fox, 'Pagans and Christians', Viking, 1986
- Robin Lane Fox, 'Alexander the Great', Allen Lane, 1973
- Walter Voigtlander, 'Antike aktuell. Didyma und Milet im Modell', Deutschen Architekturmeseums, 1986
- Herodotus, 'Histories', Wordsworth Editions, 1996
- Seutonius, 'The Twelve Caesars', Penguin Group, 1957
- Richard Dawkins, 'The God Delusion', Bantam Press, 2006
- Judith Herrin, 'Byzantium. The Surprising Life of a Medieval Empire', Allen Lane, 2007
- Tom Holland, 'Persian Fire', Little and Brown, 2005
- Ed. Simon Price and Emily Kearns, 'The Oxford Dictionary of Classical Myth & Religion', Oxford University Press, 2003
- Helga Bumke and Jan Breder, 'Die Kulte von Didyma im Licht neu entdeckter Bauten', Antike Welt 2016
- Helga Bumke, 'Aktuelle Forschungen in Didyma', Der Anschnitt, 2015
- Helga Bumke, Jan Breder, Ivonne Kaiser, Bettina Reichardt and Ulf Weber, 'Didyma. Bericht uber die Arbeiten der Jahre 2010-2013', Deutsches Archaeologisches Institut, 2015
- Marjorie Caygill, 'A-Z Companion to the Collections', The British Museum Press, 1999

- Kurt A. Raaflaub (Editor), Hans van Wees (Editor), 'A Companion to Archaic Greece', Wiley-Blackwell, 2012
- Theodor Wiegand, 1941-58. 'Didyma. The prime archaeological report', 2 vols. in 4, Berlin
- Pausanias,'Description of Greece', translation W.H.S. Jones and H.A. Ormerod, 1918
- Hans Waltenberg, Wolfgang Gleissberg, 'Das Rätsel von Didyma und seine astronomische Lösung', Stern und Weltrum, 1968
- Herbert W. Parke, 'The temple of Apollo at Didyma: the building and its function', Journal of Hellenic Studies 106:121-131, 1986
- Iamblichus, 'On the mysteries (De mysteriis)', ed. Gustav Parthey, Teubner, 1857
- David Moore Robinson, 'Greek and Latin inscriptions from Asia Minor', American Philological Association, 1926
- Alexander Herda, 'Der Apollon-Delphinios-Kult in Milet und die Neujahrsprozession nach Didyma. Ein neuer Kommentar der Molpoi-Satzung', Milesische Forschungen, Mainz, 2006

Printed in Dunstable, United Kingdom

63442027R00088